THE
RICH

Other Books by William Davis

Three Years Hard Labour
Merger Mania
Money Talks
Have Expenses, Will Travel
It's No Sin to be Rich
Money in the 1980s
The Rich: a Study of the Species
Fantasy: A Practical Guide to Escapism
The Corporate Infighter's Handbook
The Super Salesman's Handbook
The Innovators
Children of the Rich
The Lucky Generation: a Positive View of the 21st Century
Great Myths of Business
The Alien – an Autobiography
How to be British

THE
RICH

A NEW STUDY OF THE SPECIES

– WILLIAM DAVIS –

Icon Books

Published in the UK in 2006 by
Icon Books Ltd, The Old Dairy,
Brook Road, Thriplow,
Cambridge SG8 7RG
email: info@iconbooks.co.uk
www.iconbooks.co.uk

Sold in the UK, Europe, South Africa and Asia
by Faber & Faber Ltd, 3 Queen Square,
London WC1N 3AU
or their agents

Distributed in the UK, Europe, South Africa and Asia
by TBS Ltd, TBS Distribution Centre, Colchester Road
Frating Green, Colchester CO7 7DW

Published in Australia in 2006
by Allen & Unwin Pty Ltd,
PO Box 8500, 83 Alexander Street,
Crows Nest, NSW 2065

Distributed in Canada by
Penguin Books Canada,
90 Eglinton Avenue East, Suite 700,
Toronto, Ontario M4P 2YE

ISBN-10: 1-84046-766-5
ISBN-13: 978-1840467-66-6

Typesetting by
Hands Fotoset

Printed and bound in the UK by
Cromwell Press

CONTENTS

*If a man's after money, he's money mad; if he keeps it, he's a
    capitalist; if he spends it, he's a playboy.
If he doesn't get it, he's a ne'er-do-well; if he doesn't try to get it,
    he lacks ambition.
If he gets it without working for it, he's a parasite; and if he
    accumulates it after a lifetime of hard work, people call
    him a fool who never got anything out of life.*

Anonymous

INTRODUCTION

'The rich are different from you and me', F. Scott Fitzgerald is supposed to have told Ernest Hemingway, who must have noticed that himself. What he actually said was that the *very* rich are different. He explained why:

> They possess and enjoy early, and it does something to them, makes them soft where we are hard, and cynical where we are trustful, in a way that, unless you are born rich, it is difficult to understand. They think, deep in their hearts, that they are better than we are because we have had to discover the compensations and refuges of life for ourselves. Even when they enter deep into our world or sink below us, they still think they are better than we are.

He was, of course, referring to people who had inherited their wealth, not to the self-made millionaires he met in Hollywood, who were as hard as nails. So here is a basic point that needs to be made before you read on: the very rich are not only different from the rest of us but also unlike each

1

other. There are many gradations, they make their money in different ways, and they spend it in different ways.

I have met people who have never done a day's work and others whose entrepreneurial efforts, and visionary concepts, have helped to change the world. I know rich people who are stingy and others who are generous; many have given millions to charity.

One can only guess what Fitzgerald would have made of J.K. Rowling, who escaped penury as a single mother in Edinburgh by writing about a character she called Harry Potter while sitting in local cafés. The Potter books and films are estimated to have earned her more than £500 million. 'J.K. Rowling is different from you and me', would have been an accurate verdict.

Some of my friends accuse me of being 'obsessed' with the rich. As far as they are concerned, the rich are an odious lot – greedy and unscrupulous. 'Why', they ask, 'do you want to write about them?' The short answer is that I find them fascinating, and society's attitude to them no less so. The drive to get rich is a powerful force and the use of wealth is an important factor in human society. It has always been so, and will always be so.

For years, high-minded intellectuals projected their fantasies of utopia onto the Soviet Union and its satellite states in Europe. They were in love with the *idea* of an egalitarian society and became ardent disciples of Karl Marx, who claimed to know how it could be brought about.

(Marx, ironically, relied on support from a rich friend while he was working on what he once described as 'this whole economic shit'. His wife, Jenny, also had misgivings. 'I wish', she said, 'that dear Karl could have spent some time acquiring capital instead of merely writing about it'.)

The theories of 'dear Karl' have become thoroughly discredited because everyone knows what happened when communist rulers sought to turn them into reality. The poor remained poor, intellectuals were persecuted, and the people at the top of this ugly pile lived in regal splendour. Millions of Soviet citizens had to endure decades of misery until the rotten edifice collapsed.

Capitalism is far from perfect. There are injustices in our society which conscientious people simply will not tolerate. No one would quarrel with the contention that people should have equal opportunity, but there is a difference between opportunity and flat equality, between fairness and the dogmatic insistence on equality of *result*.

Communism has never got anywhere in Britain and America because the watchword has always been liberty, not equality. A free society – that is, liberal capitalism – is the only system that can uphold and protect individual rights. This is still what matters for most of us, and it includes the right to make serious money within the legal framework established by democratically elected governments.

Older readers will recall that in the 1960s and 70s many British politicians, academics, and trade union leaders took a different view. They did not like communism but felt that something had to be done about the rich. A Labour chancellor, Denis Healey, famously threatened to make them 'howl with anguish'. He later claimed to have been misquoted, but he imposed confiscatory levels of taxation. Billions were wasted on propping up loss-making industries. The economy did not improve – indeed, Britain went from one crisis to another. Poverty did not disappear. Many rich people left the country. Others decided that there was no point in working hard, and taking risks, if the Treasury was going to grab up to 97 per cent of their income.

All this changed when Margaret Thatcher became Prime Minister. She and cabinet colleagues like Geoffrey Howe and Nigel Lawson set out to 'roll back the frontiers of the State'.

They recognised that wealth has to be created before it can be distributed, and that it was mainly up to the private sector to achieve that aim. Tax cuts and the privatisation of state-owned entities transformed the economy. Their 'entrepreneurial revolution' made many of us feel that, with effort, we all stood a good chance of getting rich. Thousands of people, including me, started their own business.

Socialists still maintain that the Thatcher years were all about greed. There was certainly an element of that, but the charge is unjust. Even the present Labour government accepts the need to create an enterprise culture. Tony Blair has frequently denounced 'the snobbery shown to people who make money'. In one of his speeches he pledged to 'tear down the barriers to upward mobility' and help to change the 'unhealthy public attitudes to self-made businessmen and women'. Looking back, he said that there was 'something fundamentally anti-meritocratic about our culture. The old right-wing elite regarded entrepreneurs as beneath them. The left regarded them as anti-social. When we should have been hugely proud of our successful entrepreneurs, we tended simply to wait until they fell flat on their face and if possible help them do it.' Gordon Brown says that he wants Britain to be more like America – a country that has always encouraged the belief that there is nothing wrong with being rich, or trying to get rich. He is, at heart, Old Labour, but he is also a realist who understands the importance of wealth creation.

Many people find it hard to go along with this approach. The government's main duty, they insist, is to 'narrow the gap between the rich and the poor'. What they forget, or choose to ignore, is that it already spends vast sums on the welfare state, particularly the National Health Service. The money has to come from somewhere. The usual argument is that 'the rich can pay', but even if they were to be taxed much more heavily, the revenue would fall well short of what is required to meet the escalating costs.

Much of the resentment is based on envy, though few of the critics are prepared to admit it. The immediate emotional response to a lucrative business deal, or even a pay rise, is that in some unsavoury way, the people involved have got away with something they shouldn't.

There is an enduring myth that all wealth is accumulated by exploitation – that if someone gains, someone else loses. This may be true of the stock market, or horse racing, or a poker game, but it is certainly not true of most everyday transactions. If I buy a new suit, or a car, or a watch, it is a voluntary act that I enter into, in the full knowledge that the retailer expects to make a profit. I don't mind, because I want those things and am willing to pay for them. We may argue about the price, but both of us gain something by the exchange.

The wealth of a Bill Gates or Philip Green does not diminish my wealth or anyone else's. The money they spend on luxuries is theirs, not mine.

Society is not enriched by reducing everyone to the lowest common denominator. I find it hard to see any reason for that kind of strategy, and for abusive terms like 'stinking rich' and 'filthy rich', other than envy or the flaunting of moral superiority. The aim, surely, must be to level up rather than down – to encourage people to create wealth, and enjoy its benefits, rather than to impose equality by government decree.

Egalitarians often appeal to an undefined, and undefinable, notion of 'social justice'. They argue that the rich should be taxed more heavily because 'they are not paying their fair share'. But they don't specify how one knows what a fair share would be, and they don't question why so much of the revenue collected by the state is used to pay for a growing army of bureaucrats. What does *that* have to do with 'social justice'?

The most vehement criticism tends to be aimed at the alleged 'fat cats' – the chief executives of large corporations. Everyone feels entitled to moralise and judge, especially people who work in the public sector. The irony is that few executives qualify for inclusion on 'rich lists'. The average term of a CEO is only four years, so they don't have much time to accumulate serious wealth unless they are also major shareholders in the company.

There is less envy of entrepreneurs and of people like Elton John, Mick Jagger and David Beckham, who often earn far more. We don't call *them* fat cats.

This brings me to another basic point: the rich are no longer an exclusive club. Its membership today includes pop stars, fashion designers and models, chefs, actors, footballers and media folk. Many people have become wealthy because the value of their homes has soared. (A record number of 60,000 families in Britain are now 'property millionaires', living in homes worth at least £1 million.)

But, of course, a million isn't what it used to be. Inflation is a great deceiver. When Frank Sinatra asked 'Who wants to be a millionaire?' in the musical *High Society*, it was still possible to 'wallow in champagne and have flunkeys everywhere'. Not now.

According to the private bank Coutts, a million pounds buys five times less than it did 25 years ago. It says that you would need to be a 'thrillionaire', with three times as much money to your name, to have the same lifestyle. It defines this as owning a five-bedroom house with two staff, two luxury cars, an apartment and a yacht in St-Tropez, and an annual expenditure of £31,000 on eating out and holidays.

I doubt if even £3 million would be enough. Many houses cost more than that and are expensive to maintain. Rich people's flunkeys expect to be well paid, and a second home in the South of France would be another million. You couldn't get a proper yacht for less that that, and you would have to fork out a considerable sum each year to run it. If you want to send your children to a private school it would set you back £50,000.

Keep in mind that wealth is not the same as income. If you make good money and spend it, after the Treasury has taken its share, you are not getting any wealthier. You are just living well. Wealth is what you accumulate, or inherit, not what you spend. Many people who display a high-consumption lifestyle have few income-producing assets. They want instant gratification and assume that they will continue to earn big money. Some do, but it cannot always be taken for granted.

The numbers so often quoted in the media are also deceptive because they tend to ignore taxes and debts. What counts is net worth – the sum of all your assets minus your liabilities. If you have borrowed a lot of money you could even be on the minus side. Another factor is that the figures are usually based on assets which fluctuate in value, such as shares and property, or which are hard to pin down, like land and art treasures. They are ultimately worth only what others are willing to pay for them.

Many rich people prefer to keep their financial affairs secret. The late Malcolm Forbes, who was the first publisher to compile a rich list, once told me that there were two kinds – those who were eager to be included (and complained if they were not), and those who begged him not to mention their names because they feared that it would make them a target for criminals.

We plainly need a new definition of 'rich'. Britain's 'wealth management industry' has divided them into four grades:

At the bottom are the 'mass affluent' – people with at

least £150,000 to invest over and above the value of their homes.

Next are the 'high net worth' individuals, with a clear £660,000. They represent 0.7 per cent of the population.

Third are the 'ultra-high net worth' people – those with £6.6 million, not counting their homes. There are 135,000 in that category, according to Tulip Financial Research.

Fourth are the 'super-rich', the thousand wealthiest people in the country. The *Sunday Times* 'rich list' says to qualify you must have assets of £60 million, and each year the bar is raised higher. There are 54 billionaires, but of these, twenty have come to live in Britain from overseas and also have residences and business interests elsewhere. The top ten include three Indians, two Russians, and two Scandinavians.

You may well disagree with the classifications. They are interesting but don't tell us *why* people want to be rich or anything about their lives.

There are many different motives. Childhood experiences, I have found, tend to play a significant role. Many self-made tycoons are driven by memories of what it was like to be poor – they have never quite managed to shake off their phobia. Others are deeply influenced by their schooldays. The system aroused their competitive drive and it has been kept in high gear ever since. Money has taken the place of marks, prizes and degrees: it is the symbolic equivalent of the awards they tried so hard to get. Those who did badly at school have a great urge to prove that they were misjudged. 'I'll show them', they resolved in their youth, and they spend most of their adult life doing just that.

Many, of course, also like to have expensive status symbols and enjoy the flattery and influence that wealth can buy. Last, but not least, there is the thrill of the chase – the pleasure to be had from outsmarting rivals, acquiring the treasured possession of others, and building an empire. Money as such has ceased to be important: it's simply the yardstick by which the world judges success, a way of 'keeping the score'.

For me, it has always meant freedom of choice: the ability to decide how and where I want to live, freedom to do the kind of work I like, freedom to embark on ventures without having to ask a sceptical boss for permission. I have never wanted to be shackled to a desk in the HQ of a big corporation and get caught up in tiresome office politics.

People who start their own business, as I did, generally have the same reasons. They work long hours and take considerable risks. There is a high failure rate. But they like to be independent and, if they succeed, there is a real sense of achievement as well as financial reward.

I realise that not everyone wants to be an entrepreneur. It is perfectly feasible to lead a good life working for someone else, devoting as much time as possible to the family, and perhaps taking up an interesting hobby. Money is not the only yardstick of success. Many people are engaged in activities which may not be lucrative but which provide personal satisfaction and enrich others in the process. Doctors, teachers, musicians and scientists are obvious examples. I strongly believe, however, that people should be allowed to make a fortune through their own efforts if that is what they wish to do.

We are all familiar with the old cliché that 'money doesn't buy happiness'. Perhaps, but many of us would like to find out for ourselves. The expression tends to be used most often by people who reckon they have little chance of getting rich unless they hit the jackpot in the National Lottery. They console themselves with the thought that the rich are miserable. It is a ridiculous assumption. Some are unhappy, but not because they are loaded. There are other reasons: poor health, troublesome relationships, or the inability to come to terms with the fact that they are not immortal.

The dichotomy between wealth and happiness is entirely false. Life is what individuals make of it, as it has always been. The truth is that many people who show such public disdain for wealth are hypocrites. They would *like* to be rich but are not prepared to make the necessary effort to get there. This is why so many gamble – in betting shops, casinos, at racecourses, on the lottery, on television, and on the internet. It is the dream of instant, easy wealth that makes Britain's national lottery so popular.

Launched in 1994, it has created more than 1,800 millionaires to date. Some have won as much as £10 million. I don't object, but it is surely fair to question whether they are more 'deserving' than those of us who chose to do it the hard way.

I fully accept that the pursuit of wealth has its ugly side. There is nothing admirable about people who seek to enrich themselves through financial scams and drug dealing. Avarice is unattractive and crime of any sort is unforgivable. But there are many positive stories which merit inclusion in a book like this, and which I hope will inspire other ambitious entrepreneurs.

The Rich is not an academic treatise and I did not set out to write a polemic. My aim was to give you an insight into a world I have come to know well in more than half a century as a financial journalist and to pass on some of the lessons I have learned from my own experience. The book has a strong international flavour because I wanted to take a global view of the species. According to *Forbes* magazine, there are almost

800 dollar billionaires. The United States has by far the largest number, followed by Germany, Russia, Japan and Britain. But league tables don't really matter: what fascinates me is how they got there and how they use their wealth. In short, this is primarily a study of human behaviour.

CHAPTER 1

THE INHERITORS

Americans have an irreverent term for people who have inherited their wealth – they are said to belong to the 'lucky sperm club'. An accident of birth has given them everything they could wish for. They can do what they like, where and when they like, without worrying about the cost. That, at least, is the public perception and there is a great deal of truth in it. But it's by no means the whole story.

There is a considerable difference between Old Money and wealth which has been newly created by entrepreneurial effort. Old Money (also known as 'ancestral funding') is handed on from one generation to the next. It is a patrimony with a present and a future, literally or figuratively held in trust. It produces an income and a set of obligations – to the family and to the perpetuation of a certain way of life.

British aristocrats have traditionally preserved their estates by the ruthless application of the principle of primogeniture, whereby the oldest son inherits virtually everything. It was reckoned to be the best way of ensuring that the estate would not be broken up. In return, he promised to take good care of it.

Some welcomed the task; others saw it as an unwanted burden. It isn't easy, these days, to pay for the upkeep and repair of an ancestral pile. Many have been handed over to the National Trust. Others have been sold to the nouveau riche, including wealthy foreigners, or have become tourist attractions, conference venues and even theme parks.

Some fortunes have been dissipated through careless administration, unwise marriages, and bad investments. Many aristocrats lost large sums of money when the Lloyd's insurance market came close to collapse in the 1990s. Others have indulged in reckless spending. John Hervey, the 7th Marquess of Bristol, squandered a £30 million inheritance on drugs and high living. Twice jailed for drug offences, he ended up in a rented farmhouse on the edge of a 4,000-acre estate that had been in the family for 500 years. He had assets of only £5,000 when he was found dead in 1999 at the age of 44, and nothing was left after liabilities, including funeral expenses, were taken into account.

In America, too, many families have seen a sharp decline in the wealth that should have been preserved for the next generation. It is one of the main reasons why extensive use is made of trusts and family holding companies.

The purpose of these devices is to keep principal intact and to hold inheritance taxes to a minimum. A wealthy individual may create a single large trust for the benefit of all his descendants. More often, a few key family members serve as trustees of a series of separate trusts for the benefit of many different members of the clan. They tend to bristle with clauses and stipulations designed to meet every contingency. Many are so-called 'generation-skipping trusts'. Under these arrangements, the children are usually entitled to receive all the income for life; the grandchildren, who are generally the remaindermen of the trust, get the assets only after the death of the last surviving beneficiary. When principal is paid out, it is often in dribbling instalments through the recipient's lifetime. It is a ploy that was developed primarily to protect fortunes from gift and estate taxes, but it also helps to prevent the dissipation of capital through the exercise of immature judgement. The first generation cannot disturb the principal and the next generation does not get all of it – or sometimes any of it – until its members are quite advanced in age. At that point many of them have locked the principal back in new trusts for the benefit of the next two generations.

Trusts sometimes lead to bitter family feuds, but by and large they have served Old Money well. The children of the rich may not have freely available capital (as most of us tend to assume they have), but they are provided with a handsome income. They do not have to get a job, start a business, or do any of the other things to which the less fortunate devote their lives. If they wish, they can simply sit back and collect the interest or dividends. There is no financial incentive to do anything else.

It is this state of affairs, envied by the outside world, which so often results in an aimless existence. Because there is no need for effort, it is all too easy to become lethargic or to spend one's life in the frivolous pursuit of pleasure.

Many Old Money families recognise the danger and try to involve their offspring in work which, although it may not produce financial rewards, is nevertheless of value to the clan or to the community. This is where Old Money's concept of duty comes into play again. It may mean the preservation of a stately home or estate, or a close involvement in one or more of the family's philanthropic enterprises.

Private foundations are not as old as trusts but they have come to play an increasingly important role in the management of wealth. They enable the rich to escape taxes and to maintain control (at least to some extent) over corporations in which they are major stockholders while, at the same time, getting involved in all kinds of useful activities – museums, art galleries, colleges, medical research, conservation programmes, and so on. Even a small foundation can have a considerable impact at the local level.

Because the accumulation of cultural and social capital is considered to be important, Old Money families devote much time and effort to ensuring that their children understand, accept, and implement the code of behaviour which has been passed on with the financial benefits. They send them to expensive schools which can be relied on to teach essential attributes like good manners, sportsmanship (i.e. the ability to lose without throwing a tantrum) and an appreciation of opera and the ballet.

There is a nice story about the child of a wealthy banker who, in her first year, was asked to write an essay on poverty. 'There once was a very poor family', she began. 'Everyone in the family was poor. The butler was poor, the chauffeur was poor, the maids were poor …' Apocryphal, perhaps, but it's not difficult to imagine how a sheltered upbringing, continued at school, can lead to a false perception of everyday realities.

Girls are expected to learn how to make endless small talk without appearing to get bored and to acquire skills like riding and dancing. Boys will be introduced to another Old Money pastime – shooting. British aristocrats have an insatiable urge to kill birds, and male heirs will be taught how to bag an impressive number of them. Fox-hunting was also popular until the Labour government passed a law against it.

Society balls, on both sides of the Atlantic, generally have a dual function. One is to raise funds for charitable causes. The other is to enable young members of the family to meet 'suitable' partners of the opposite sex. It is the parental alternative to dangerous places like discos, where they are liable to get involved with undesirables like plumbers and secretaries from working-class areas. Old Money people recognise that they have to move with the times, but they feel the need to draw the line somewhere.

Suitable young men and women may be invited to a week-end house party, which in London generally means going off to 'the country'. There may be up to a dozen guests, which gives parents the opportunity to study the friends of their children without being too obvious about it. They must not seem overly impressed by the splendour of the surroundings (the 'right people' take such things for granted) and they must not plead ignorance or lack of skill if asked to participate in Old Money sports or parlour games. Proficiency in bridge or chess is also considered to be a useful attribute. The conversation usually ranges around the shared interests of the rich: horses, dogs, gardens, servant problems, and taxes. Occasionally a guest will express a dissenting view but a spirited display of independence is bad form.

The most serious offence, even in America, is to brag about the wealth of one's family or how much money has been made from the latest deal. The upper classes are as interested in the subject as everyone else, but it is simply not done to talk about it on social occasions.

This convention is also upheld in exclusive clubs. For as long as anyone can remember, they have prohibited conversations about business. Their purpose is to provide a civilised milieu in which like-minded people can meet, dine, read, play cards, or just doze in a comfortable armchair.

Although the 'gentleman's club' originated in London, it is one of the enduring legacies of Empire around the world. India and other former colonies have their own versions. So does the United States. Some of the most venerable clubs are in New York. They now have female members, and have been infiltrated by New Money, but applications are carefully vetted.

It is, by and large, Old Money behaviour that is still widely regarded as the epitome of 'British style'. My rich American friends know exactly what they mean by it. For them, it's not just a matter of possessions or aristocratic titles. As they see it, we have an enviable capacity for understatement. We do not feel a compelling need to have the biggest of everything. We do not hustle, we do not push, we are not aggressive. We are formal: we keep our jackets and ties on even if it's very hot; we dress up for dinner; and we call our political enemies 'honourable gentlemen'. We do not worship the new merely because it is new. We hang on to the old because we are used to it, like it, and believe in tradition.

It's difficult for most of us to accept that such generalisations add up to a realistic portrait of Britain in the 21st century. Most self-made millionaires would certainly reject the whole thing as out of date and superficial. He or she hustles and loves the new. It may not be Old Money style, but it is assuredly British.

Class still plays a role, but the social divide is not what it used to be. Young people from all walks of life study together at universities like Oxford and Cambridge; marriage outside one's 'class' has become commonplace; pop stars like Elton John and Mick Jagger have been given knighthoods; and many years have passed since an aristocrat last occupied 10 Downing Street. We have more than our share of snobs, but they are just as likely to be found in academic and literary circles than among the old upper class.

The nouveau riche are more likely to involve their offspring in business than Old Money families. Some are given posts in the family company, but today it may be publicly owned and run by professional managers, so any pretender to the corporate throne had better have talent. The same goes for a career in the City; there is little room for the well-bred amateur.

Many first generation multi-millionaires say that they don't feel under any obligation to pass on their wealth. Paul Sykes, a Barnsley miner's son who made an estimated £500 million in property, told the *Sunday Times* that he will not leave his children a penny, even though there is no family rift. 'They will have much more satisfaction and fulfilment by using their own initiatives, creative abilities and efforts to generate their success in life. To be fed with a silver spoon and have life on a plate is debilitating for a young person. They need the challenge of life, the challenge of success or failure.'

Anita Roddick, the founder of Body Shop, has also vowed to give away her entire fortune. Sam, her 35-year-old daughter, displays no rancour at her decision. 'Actually', she says, 'it's a relief. If the money was divided between family members I suppose it would be natural to equate the amount that you were left with the amount that you were loved, which makes it very complicated and emotional. So if my mum had said to me, "I'm not leaving the money to you but I've decided to give it all to a distant cousin", then I would have found that offensive. But giving it all to charity is different. You can't really argue about someone giving their money away, can you?'

Sam runs a sex shop in London's Covent Garden and many other young people from affluent New Money families have also started their own ventures. They usually have two things going for them: seed capital and influential contacts. Not all, however, have what it takes to succeed.

The late Robert Maxwell informed his children in 1988 that his wealth would go to charity. His son Kevin told me at the time that he welcomed the decision. 'I do not believe that a child has an inalienable right to inherit', he said. 'I am very comfortable that I have to fend for myself and may well do so through my own endeavours. I have no God-given right to be a billionaire because Dad is.'

Kevin, who has an Oxford degree, had already worked for another company in America but agreed to return to Britain when Robert offered him a senior position in the family business. It was to have disastrous consequences. Robert's empire, by then a public company, collapsed and he was found dead, floating in the sea where he had been cruising on his yacht. Even now, many years later, no one really knows what happened – was it suicide, a heart attack, or murder? What is known is that he left an appalling mess. The empire's debts had soared to £2.7 billion and, in desperation, he had raided its pension funds. Kevin and his brother were arrested and had to endure a lengthy trial. They were eventually acquitted because all the misdeeds were attributed to their domineering father. But Kevin ended up as Britain's biggest bankrupt, owing £400 million.

When he was discharged, he launched a new business venture but it also ran into problems. In 2005, he faced another humiliation: opening up the family home, which he had been forced to sell to repay a loan secured against it, to bargain hunters in an everything-must-go jumble sale. A kilt and sporran that had belonged to Robert (who was born in Czechoslovakia) were snapped up by a museum for £750, but Kevin could not bring himself to part with his father's old army uniform. It is the only inheritance of value which he may, one day, want to pass on to one of his seven children.

LUCKY GERALD

One aristocrat who doesn't have to worry about money is Gerald Cavendish Grosvenor, 6th Duke of Westminster. He has an estimated fortune of more than £5 billion.

The family's prize possession is a large part of fashionable Belgravia, acquired by an ancestor when it was marshland. The Duke also own estates in Lancashire, Cheshire and

Scotland, and is an active property developer with interests around the world.

Gerald is an amiable, unassuming six-footer who travels thousands of miles each year on business. He was born and bred on a farm in Northern Ireland, and first learned that he was going to inherit the Westminster money when he was fifteen. It had actually been put in his name much earlier, but no one had seen fit to tell him. (He is still grateful for this rather than annoyed: it meant, he says, that he had 'an infinitely happier childhood'.) To minimise death duties, the legendary four-times-married second Duke had drawn up a canny will before his death in 1953. It bypassed the elderly heirs, who became 3rd, 4th and 5th Dukes, in favour of baby Gerald.

His formal training for the role was virtually non-existent. His father never even sat down with him to discuss it. He attended Sunningdale and Harrow, but only managed to get two O levels and left school at eighteen to work on ranches in British Columbia and New Zealand. When he returned to London, he worked for a short time with a firm of estate agents, but then his father had a stroke and Gerald assumed the reins at 21. He was about as well qualified for the task as the office boy, but happily there were older, very experienced trustees to guide him.

In 1978, he married nineteen-year-old Natalia Phillips, a former *Vogue* secretary and direct descendant of the Russian poet Alexander S. Pushkin. Their honeymoon was spent touring the various overseas properties; a year later he became Duke of Westminster in his own right.

Like most Old Money people, he does not feel that the inheritance is his to spend. He firmly believes in the principle that his mandate is to hand over to the next generation a family estate that is in better shape than the one he was given. 'The pull of history is very strong', he says. 'People tend to ignore it or just think it's something to commercialise, but it's a very stabilising factor. And it's my duty to continue it.'

He and Natalia have four children, including a son, who is his heir apparent. The family home is Eaton Hall, a country mansion set within a large park near Chester. The 13,000-acre estate has belonged to the Grosvenors since the 15th century, but the house served as a hospital in both world wars and as an officer cadet training school from 1946 to 1960. The main part was later demolished by the trustees, who put up a modern building. It contains a fine collection of furniture and paintings, but is not open to the public.

One of the Duke's most ambitious plans is to turn Liverpool into paradise. He has acquired 42 acres in the city centre and is spending £750 million on a new village that will include an upmarket shopping centre, hotels, and apartments. It will be enclosed within its own boundaries and policed by US-style 'quartermasters', or sheriffs, who will be allowed to remove 'undesirables' by force. It was his decision to call it Project Paradise.

Gerald Grosvenor has long been a part-time soldier. He joined the Territorial Army as a private in 1970 and later became an officer. In earlier times he might have gone on to lead his troops into battle, but he settled readily enough for wearing a uniform on weekend exercises. He was made colonel-in-chief of several regiments and is now a major-general. He is also involved with many charities and in 2005 became Chancellor of the University of Chester.

With so much going on, one wonders how he manages to find time for the recreations listed in his *Who's Who* entry: shooting, fishing and scuba diving. He obviously doesn't have to work, but says that he enjoys it. 'Challenge is the thing', he once told me. 'That and the satisfaction – however trite it may sound – of doing it right.'

Glorious Goodwood

Dukes like Gerald Grosvenor are entitled to be addressed as 'Your Grace'. It can be confusing. There is a nice story about a little boy who was introduced to the Duke of Sutherland and called him 'Sir', to the consternation of his father, who dug him in the ribs and whispered: 'No, boy, Your Grace.' The child looked the Duke in the eye and said: 'For what we are about to receive, may the Lord make us truly thankful.'

Gerald would find that funny; so, I'm sure, would the other members of that dwindling band of aristocrats.

One of the most enterprising is Charles March, otherwise known as the Earl of March and Kinrara, heir to the 10th Duke of Richmond, a direct descendant of King Charles II. He runs one of the most famous country estates in Britain – Goodwood.

Like so many others of his class, Charles was sent to Eton to get the 'right sort' of education. He hated it, and left at the age of sixteen to become a photographer. He went on to work in advertising and, by all accounts, was very good at his job. But duty called.

Originally purchased by the first Duke as a hunting lodge in 1697, Goodwood House is set in 12,000 acres of land. It was extensively refurbished by architect James Wyatt a century later, and his stamp of ornate grandeur is everywhere. Another Duke was so keen on horses that he built a racecourse: Glorious Goodwood, a five-day meet held annually at the end of July, dates back to 1814. In the 1950s and 60s it also became renowned as the venue for an annual motor-sport event. When Charles took over the estate from his father in 1994, he was determined to preserve its sporting heritage. He launched a Festival of Speed, which soon began to attract top drivers, and what he says is 'by far the biggest historic race meeting in the world', the Goodwood Revival. For three days in

September, the circuit is awash with historic cars and motor-bikes, attended by a vast crowd with almost everyone dressed in period clothes.

As an astute promoter, his Lordship is well aware of the need to please both sexes. 'Ladies will love this!' he says on his website, 'this' meaning that he will 'bring couture to the Revival in a way that hasn't been achieved before'. It may sound patronising but it works.

Like Gerald Grosvenor, he is often asked why he took on such a huge responsibility. His answer is much the same: it was both a duty and a challenge. Managing the estate is a task he shares with his wife, Janet, their three children and a daughter from his first marriage. He says that he doesn't want to put too much pressure on the next generation: 'If my son doesn't want to do it, that's fine. I hope he does, but if he doesn't enjoy it he won't do well at it.'

What many women find objectionable – and, in my view, rightly so – is the idea that only a *son* is fit to deal with the challenges faced by Old Money in the 21st century. Many male heirs are plainly not in the same league as Gerald Grosvenor and Charles March. I have met some who are as dumb as Bertie Wooster, the toff immortalised by P.G. Wodehouse in his entertaining and perceptive novels, and I wouldn't trust them to run a fish and chip shop, let alone an estate.

CHAPTER 2

ROYAL LIVES

Royalty is in a class by itself. There are people who have far more money than most of the world's remaining royal families, but they don't have the inherited status which sets kings, queens and princes apart.

Membership of the world's most exclusive club has always carried dangers as well as privileges. The French executed their last king and the British beheaded Charles I. In Russia, the Bolsheviks shot the entire royal family. Germany toppled the Kaiser after he lost the 1914–18 war, and more recently a number of other monarchs have been unceremoniously deposed and forced into exile – Umberto of Italy, Constantine of Greece, the Shah of Iran.

No one can predict with any degree of accuracy how many royals will survive as heads of state in the next twenty or thirty years, but the institution is far from dead. Spain actually revived it after the long years of Franco's rule.

Europe's kings and queens have managed to adapt themselves to changing circumstances and will no doubt continue to do so. They are rich, but not in the same league as the King of Saudi Arabia and the Sultan of Brunei. Even the Aga Khan has more money than the royals of countries like Denmark, Sweden and Norway. A direct descendant of the Prophet Mohammad, he is the 49th hereditary Imam of some 20 million Ismaili Muslims, who worship him as their 'bringer of light'.

The Aga, a British citizen, is very different from the dour Muslim leaders we so often see on TV. Best known to gossip columnists as a playboy, he owns 600 racehorses, three jets, several yachts, homes in five countries, and a priceless collection of jewels and antiques. His business interests include hotels, a newspaper, factories and an airline. He also runs a charitable foundation.

Queen Margrethe of Denmark learned of her destiny at the age of thirteen, when a referendum overturned the Salic law which said that only males could inherit the throne. 'My first reaction was utter terror', she said later. 'Then my parents made me see that there could be no higher service that I could render to my country. Now my job never ends. It will last my entire life.'

While studying at the London School of Economics, she met French diplomat Count Laborde de Monpezat, and they got to know each other better in Scotland. They decided to get married and he became Henrik, Prince of Denmark. The Danes were not sure about him at first. 'Some people', he recalled when I interviewed him in Copenhagen, 'thought it was an insult to Danish manhood that the heir to the throne should marry a Frenchman. So they were quite aggressive to begin with. I said at the time that I had the most difficult job in the world and I meant it. Things are much better now.' He talked with some pride about his vineyards in France, which he had kept, but said that they tried to live like 'an ordinary family'. Their palaces, he pointed out, were not theirs – 'they belong to the nation'.

King Juan Carlos of Spain was born in exile and had no

reason to believe, as a child, that he would one day become his country's head of state. He did not see Spain until the age of nine. General Franco was the undisputed ruler after the Civil War, which ended in 1939. He said that the monarchy would be restored eventually, but did not name a date and did not make it clear who would be king. Juan Carlos was not next in line; his grandfather had renounced his rights in favour of his third son, Don Juan, the Count of Barcelona and father of Juan Carlos. Franco, however, did not want Don Juan to succeed him. He was too liberal and, in any event, too long out of Spain. So the ageing dictator took the boy prince under his wing and groomed him as a possible successor – though it was not until 1969, when he was thirty, that he was officially declared heir to the throne. Franco remained at the helm until his death six years later. When Juan Carlos became king, he immediately gave most of his prerogatives to Parliament, which in return agreed to pay for the upkeep of the monarch. He and his family have an enviable lifestyle, but they are not as rich as some of their citizens.

The King of Sweden, Carl Gustav, is said to have inherited only about US $600,000. The state agreed to continue paying him an allowance for the performance of royal duties, but took away most of his other privileges. He has to pay taxes on his income, like any private citizen, and is also liable to customs duty on anything he brings into the country.

The last absolute rulers in Europe head tiny states like Monaco and Liechtenstein. Prince Albert of Monaco is best known because his mother was the glamorous Hollywood film star, Grace Kelly, who later died in a tragic road accident. Her death had a profound effect on the family.

Her two daughters had disastrous relationships before settling down. Albert, the heir, was educated in America and, for a time, lived in New York. He studied banking and international law, and also worked for an advertising agency.

When I met him in the family's picturesque palace, protected by ancient cannons and costumed guards, he told me that the experience had been useful but that he could never have been a banker – 'it would be terribly boring'. He thought that advertising was a 'fascinating business' but that if he had been forced to earn a living, he would probably have been in sport, education or music. He said that he had a 'strong sense of commitment' to Monaco but that he was not going to take himself too seriously – 'you must have a sense of humour in life'.

His father died in 2005 and he is now His Serene Highness, ruler of a sunny tax haven that is smaller than New York's Central Park and horribly overbuilt.

The richest monarch on the Continent is reputed to be Queen Beatrix of the Netherlands. She was two years old when the Second World War broke out and was hastily exiled, first to England and then to Canada, where she spent an idyllic five years being brought up in the Ottawa countryside. When she returned to Holland, the Princess went to an ordinary Dutch school where she was taught in a class with other children. She later studied legal science, parliamentary history, politics and sociology at the University of Leiden. Like Margrethe of Denmark, she married a foreign diplomat, Claus von Amsberg. Because he was German, he had to endure a great deal of public hostility. The Queen's personal fortune is a closely guarded secret, but she is known to have inherited considerable wealth when she came to the throne in 1980.

Queen Elizabeth is also very rich. Few people know just how large her fortune is: she has always insisted that her private funds are none of the public's business. (Her investments are handled by a secretive body known as Bank of England Nominees.) Buckingham Palace, Windsor Castle and her other official residences belong to the State, but she owns Balmoral and Sandringham in her own right. She also has an annual income of about £10 million from the Duchy of Lancaster, which enables her to support some of her relatives, buy nice clothes, make donations to charity, and run a racing stable of more than a dozen horses in training and 25 brood mares in stud. (Horses have always been her great passion. British Airways pilots still tell the story of what happened on a flight to Australia. Prince Philip eagerly accepted an invitation to join the captain in the cockpit but when he was asked if the Queen would also honour him with her presence, he is said to have replied: 'Not a chance. If it ate hay and farted she would be here like a shot, but she is not in the least bit interested in what you do.')

She has a personal collection of jewellery, much of it left to her by Queen Mary and her own mother, but the Crown Jewels are held in trust for the nation. The same goes for the Royal Collection, one of the largest and finest art collections in the world. Assembled by monarchs from Henry VIII onwards, it contains more than 7,000 paintings, 20,000 Old Masters drawings, 3,000 miniatures, and 1 million historic artefacts including furniture, sculpture, jewellery, and porcelain. The Royal yacht *Britannia* was decommissioned in 1997 and has not been replaced.

The Queen pays taxes on her income but is not expected to foot the bill for running the monarchy. The government has done so since George III surrendered the highly profitable Crown Estate in 1760.

Prince Charles has a large income from the Duchy of Cornwall. The 135,000-acre estate was created by King Edward III, the warrior monarch of the 14th century. He decided that his eldest son, the Black Prince, should enjoy a trust fund worthy of the heir to the throne and parcelled up some of his castles, manors and hamlets, largely in the counties of Devon and Cornwall, and granted them to his son with a new title: the Duke of Cornwall. There was, however, one condition. He was free to use the annual profits from his new Duchy as he liked, but at his death must pass on the estate, intact, to his own eldest son. Charles inherited it when his mother was crowned Queen, and takes a close interest in the way it is run, but he cannot touch the capital. He has extensive personal investments, but when he and the late Princess Diana were divorced he had to pay her £18 million as a settlement – the most he had ever spent on anything. He and his new wife, now the Duchess of Cornwall, live mainly at Highgrove, their house in the Cotswolds.

The Prince has never shown much interest in the accumulation of wealth. He once told me that at heart he was a complete countryman: 'I could be very happy occupying myself as a farmer.' But he accepts that it was not the life mapped out for him, and has tried to make himself useful. In an interview on American television in October 2005, he made a veiled appeal for sympathy. He said that many found it easy to dismiss him because of his privileged status and failed to recognise his achievements. Asked to pinpoint the pitfalls of being heir to the throne, he replied: 'The most important thing is to be relevant. It isn't easy, as you can imagine, because if you say anything, people will say, "It's all right for you to say that".' He explained that he tries to enrich lives through his charity and environmental projects, and added: 'I only hope that when I am dead and gone they might appreciate me a little more.' His top priority, he told the interviewer, was 'worrying about Britain and its inhabitants – that's my particular duty. I find myself born into this particular position and I am determined to make the most of it.'

When he becomes king, Charles will get most of his mother's assets (she has already made sure that other members of the family won't starve). He will be very rich but he, too, intends to preserve as much as possible for the next generation.

Princess Diana left £12 million to William and his brother Harry. They will get control of it at 25, so they won't have to rely on their father for financial support. William will also inherit the Duchy of Cornwall in due course. The big question, yet unanswered, is whether he will want the job of king when the time comes. He may well find the role of heir as difficult as Charles has done.

The lesser royals, and their children, generally have far more scope in their choice of activities than those at the very top. The one thing asked of them is that they should not bring the institution of monarchy into disrepute. They cannot afford to get drunk in public, get caught with drugs, or become involved in a financial scandal. They may tour factories, declare overseas trade fairs well and truly open, work for charity or a reputable company. They may also start their own business. Prince Edward has had a go, but it didn't work out as well as he had hoped. Viscount Linley, the son of the late Princess Margaret and twelfth in line to the throne, has fared better. He began to take an interest in carpentry while still at school and later trained as a cabinet-maker. He opened a shop in Chelsea twenty years ago and has since added one in Mayfair. His clients include many of the rich and famous on both sides of the Atlantic.

Through usually described by the press as the 'royal carpenter', he nowadays concentrates on selling the firm's products. Being the Queen's nephew has obvious advantages but he is not a snob: when we met, over lunch, he asked me to call him David and talked enthusiastically about his work. I found him unassuming and likeable – much more like his father, the photographer Lord Snowdon, than his mother, who would never let you forget that she was the Queen's sister. (Only close friends, like the late Peter Sellers, dared to call her Margaret.)

Linley has a trust fund and an inheritance from his mother

but insists that he is not as rich as people think he is – 'I wish I was', he says. He upset Princess Margaret when she was still alive by selling her beloved home on the Caribbean island of Mustique, which she had given him to avoid inheritance tax, and in June 2006 created a stir when he and his sister Lady Sarah put 800 lots of their mother's possessions under the hammer at Christie's to pay off death duties of £3 million. The auction netted £13.6 million, considerably more than the Christie's estimate. David's wife Serena also has a trust fund. She is the daughter of Viscount Petersham, heir to the 11th Earl of Harrington and owner of some prime real estate in central London. He is reputed to be worth £120 million.

Monarchists say that the institution is still needed because it supplies a sense of unity, continuity and history. It is an argument which many people find hard to accept. They resent being 'subjects' of an unelected head of state, complain about the cost of the monarchy, and regard the ceremonial as absurdly old-fashioned. But Britain and other European countries have, so far, shown little inclination to dispense with their royal families. This is mainly because they have resisted the temptation to meddle in politics (and therefore can't be held responsible for unpopular decisions) and because the public quite likes the ceremonial and the traditional.

BLACK GOLD

London's Savoy Hotel has long been a venerable British institution, so there was some concern when it was bought by a Saudi prince in 2005. Would he turn it into a gaudy palace? Londoners were all too familiar with tales of Arab excess – their fondness for kitsch and extravagant follies. Some were undoubtedly true, but many were apocryphal or based on remarks that were intended to be humorous but were taken seriously because it was assumed, wrongly, that Arabs have no sense of humour. When the Sultan of Oman's private jet was delayed at Heathrow during a strike, he sent a message to the control tower asking how much it would cost to buy the airport. It was his idea of a joke (he had been to a boarding school in England) but the press thought he meant it.

We tend to be envious of Arab wealth and because we are envious, many of us are resentful. We tell ourselves that they have done nothing to deserve all those riches; the oil was discovered by Western geologists. Saudi Arabia did not become a nation until 1932. Its founder Ibn Saud used to carry his family fortune in the saddle-bag of his camel. When he proclaimed himself king he was broke. The country would have remained of little interest to anyone if it had not emerged that it held the world's largest reserve of 'black gold'. Europe and America competed for concessions and the money rolled in.

American resentment of Arab wealth is just as great, but successive administrations have supported the royals despite their autocratic behaviour. The current president, George W. Bush, says that he wants to bring democracy to the Middle East. He claims that it was the main reason why he invaded Iraq and deposed its dictator, Saddam Hussein. He also wants to topple the regimes of Iran and Syria but has not threatened the Saudis. He doesn't really need to, because they keep assuring him that they are not anti-American.

All this could change if the turmoil in the Middle East were to lead to a revolution. It happened in Iran, where religious leaders forced the Shah into exile, and it may happen in Saudi Arabia. We should not be surprised, therefore, that the country's royals are so eager to acquire assets abroad.

We have been here before. When the princes and other rulers from the Middle East first embarked on massive foreign investments in the early 1970s, many people in the West felt uneasy. Were a handful of Arabs going to end up owning *everything*? I remember the public outcry when it was revealed that the Sultan of Brunei had acquired the Dorchester Hotel. London's dining rooms were buzzing with all kinds of rumours. The Arabs, it was said, were on the point of buying Fortnum & Mason. They were even after *The Times*, so that they could get favourable publicity for their cause. 'Arabs may buy Knightsbridge', said a headline in the *Guardian*. Questions were asked in parliament, and the government was urged to pass preventive legislation.

But by no means everyone was displeased. Bankers, stock-brokers and real estate agents made discreet trips to the Gulf to persuade the new masters that they had just the right deal for them. Even aristocrats joined in the hunt. One friend of mine, lumbered with an expensive property which no one seemed willing to buy, had a full-colour brochure printed in Arabic and bought ads in Arab newspapers. (It worked.) Others gleefully swapped tales about the fancy prices paid for London houses and flats. South Kensington became known as Saudi Kensington.

Since then, the Arabs have tended to make their investments primarily through companies and agencies run by British businessmen but, in reality, owned by them. It attracts less attention. They have done the same in America, where the terrorist attacks of 9/11 added fear to the resentment. Osama Bin Laden is a Saudi, as were the leaders of the suicide squads who hijacked planes and flew them into the twin towers of the World Trade Center and the Pentagon.

The royal who bought the Savoy, Prince Alwaleed bin Talal, is reputed to be the wealthiest member of the family, with an estimated fortune of more than £12 billion. His investment company, Kingdom Holding, also owns the George V in Paris and has major stakes in Four Seasons Hotels, Saks Fifth Avenue, and Rupert Murdoch's News Corporation.

The Prince (one of many Saudis with that title) became notorious in New York when the Mayor declined to accept a $10 million donation from him to families of 9/11 victims, after he suggested that the US was too friendly with Israel. He later gave $20 million to Harvard and another $20 million to Georgetown University, which they promised to spend on Islamic studies. He told the *New York Times* in 2005: 'I am a friend of the United States, and these days to be in the Arab world and to be a friend of the United States is a liability. But nevertheless I say it. I am a great friend.'

Other rulers have used their wealth in different ways. Sheik Mohammed bin Rashid Al Maktoum, for example, is well known in Britain for his love of horse racing (and the English social scene) but he has also played a key role in transforming Dubai into a playground for the rich.

Another conspicuous spender has been Sheik Saud Al-Thani of Qatar. A cousin of the all-powerful Emir, he was put in charge of the tiny country's National Council for Culture, Arts and Heritage. Armed with seemingly unlimited funds, he embarked on an eight-year shopping spree, forking out more than £1 billion on objects and works of art. He collected feverishly across the board: Islamic art (his greatest passion), photography, jewels, 18th-century French furniture, vintage cars, textiles, natural history books, Egyptian and Roman antiquities, and much else. 'Unlike Turkey or Egypt', he explained, 'we have no art-historical tradition. His Highness would like Qatar to become a cultivated country.'

Qatar can afford big dreams: it has plenty of oil. The Emir plans to spend £58 billion in the next few years on infrastructure and other projects to diversify the economy. Some of the other Gulf states are less fortunate. Bahrain ran out of oil some time ago and has to find other sources of revenue.

Iraq has ample reserves, but it remains to be seen who will benefit the most. The same goes for Iran. The Shah initiated some of the most advanced social programmes in the world but his regime was so corrupt, and unpopular, that religious fanatics were able to take over. Many rich Iranians, who saw this coming, transferred their assets in good time – to tax havens like Switzerland and Liechtenstein but also to Britain, France, and America.

Middle East states are not, of course, the only suppliers of oil. Russia, Nigeria and Venezuela are also significant producers. But Saudi Arabia is the most important, and if the royals can stay in power (which is by no means certain) the biggest problem for people like Prince Alwaleed will be how to spend all that money. Western countries are still top of the shopping list, but China and India offer new opportunities. They have become major customers and may give Arab investors access in return for strategic oil-supply deals.

Thirty years ago, the Saudi princes squandered petrodollar fortunes on fast cars and gambling. It was an orgy of extravagance. The new generation is a lot smarter.

CHAPTER 3

THE ENTREPRENEURS

There have always been entrepreneurs, but the label has only become respectable in recent times. In my youth they were called hustlers, adventurers, opportunists. In America the people who created great fortunes in the 19th century – men like Rockefeller, Vanderbilt and Carnegie – were known as 'robber barons'. Even now, Old Money families who live on the wealth they left behind tend to refer to the new generation of empire builders as parvenus or nouveau riche. British aristocrats may envy them but some also express contempt for their 'pushy ways'.

One of the main reasons why many of us take a different view is that, in recent decades, entrepreneurs have produced most of the new private sector jobs and innovations. Another is the revival in individualism – the quest for economic independence. More people than ever before want to do their own thing. The popular image of the entrepreneur today is that of an individual who is vital, creative, courageous.

Not everyone, of course, wants to build up a large enterprise. Many people start small and remain small. There is a difference between the person who buys a shop and the entrepreneur who develops a chain. The shopkeeper is more interested in independence than in achievement. The builder has more lofty ambitions. But both have a common desire: to be in control. Neither feels comfortable in a big organisation run by someone else.

A distinction also needs to be made between inventors and innovators. The two terms are often confused. The inventor discovers something new and useful; the innovator takes up an idea and develops it. Many talented people manage to do both, but someone who is good at inventing is not necessarily good at turning a concept into a viable commercial proposition.

One of the most intriguing aspects of America's Silicon Valley is the abundance of 'serial entrepreneurs' – people who have created and sold several companies. They identify a concept which seems to have serious potential, see it through the early stages, and then move on to the next. In Britain, venture capitalists do the same.

Entrepreneurial folklore says that they don't invest in a business until their rising greed overcomes their declining fear. In other words, they don't put money into a company unless, and until, they are convinced that there is a reasonable probability that the financial returns measure up to the risks. They generally expect to get a return of between five and ten times their initial investment in about five to seven years. In an ideal case, the company will grow rapidly and make a public offering or sell the business to a larger group. In practice, this means that venture capitalists will back only companies with first-class entrepreneurial leaders in markets that are big enough for a company to show significant growth in sales and profits. Many also hedge their bets by providing the finance in stages and syndicating the deal with others.

One of the main drawbacks in getting involved with them is that their investments tend to have all sorts of covenants and restrictions. When things go badly wrong, they exercise their rights and intervene in managing the company, often removing the founder. It is these situations which have given rise to the derogatory term 'vulture capitalists'. However, if things go well, everyone wins.

Many tend to focus increasingly on management buy-outs of all or part of a business, because they are usually more profitable than start-up companies and pay off more quickly.

In America, venture capitalists tend to be bolder. They are more likely to finance start-up and early stage businesses. Many are instrumental in the creation of the companies they back, bringing entrepreneurs and investors together to launch new enterprises. They take a Darwinian view: invest in a lot and let the fittest survive. It is not unusual for only one or two companies in a portfolio to make it to success. But the profits on the winners can be so big that it's reckoned to be worth taking the risk.

Much depends on what the stock market does at any given time. If a sector is 'hot' the game is easy, but if the market falls out of love with it, many of the people who showed such enthusiasm for new ventures withdraw their support – with devastating consequences for entrepreneurs who have come to rely on it.

There are many theories about what it takes to be a successful entrepreneur. I will return to the subject in a later chapter; meanwhile, let us consider the widely held view that entrepreneurship can be taught. Many colleges nowadays have professors of entrepreneurship who claim to have all the answers. Anita Roddick, founder of the Body Shop, is among the many people at the sharp end of business who question this assumption. She asks:

> How do you teach obsession? There is a fine line
> between the delinquent mind of the entrepreneur and

that of a crazy person. The entrepreneur's dream is almost a kind of madness, and it is almost as isolating. When you see something new, your vision usually isn't shared by others. The difference between a crazy person and the successful entrepreneur is that the latter can convince others to share the vision. That force of will is fundamental to entrepreneurship.

What could a professor know about 'the force of will'? He can conduct numerous case studies, and devise fancy theories, but how can an academic truly understand – let alone convey – the 'kind of madness' that makes all the difference?

Some years ago I wrote a book called *The Innovators*, which looked at the remarkable careers of more than a hundred people who made things happen in the 20th century. Most of them, I found, encountered the same kind of objections one still hears today. 'It can't be done. It costs too much. It's too risky. It takes too long to get returns.'

Warren Avis, who developed the airport car rental concept while still in his twenties, recalled that the objections 'ran the gamut of negative thinking. I was told that a national rental system of this type would be impossible to control. There would not be enough demand from business travellers. The cost of buying and maintaining the cars would undermine any profitability. You name it, the naysayers threw it at me.'

Fred Smith of Federal Express came up with his revolutionary idea for an overnight air-freight service back in 1965, while he was still a student at Yale. He wrote a paper about it for his economic class. His professor called it impractical and gave him a C. Six years later, Fred launched the company that won him fame and fortune.

Walt Disney found it so hard to get financial backing for his dreams that his first business venture ended in bankruptcy. He left Kansas City to try his luck in Hollywood, with just $40 in his pocket. He was commissioned to do a series of *Alice in Wonderland* comedies. He talked his older brother Roy into joining him, and he in turn persuaded an uncle to invest $500 in the new enterprise. The Disney Bros. studio was born. But they remained desperately short of money and eagerly accepted an offer to make another series, to be called *Oswald the Lucky Rabbit.* The distributors were happy with it – so happy that they stole away the Disney animators and did the job themselves. For the second time in his young life Walt had to accept defeat. He went back to Kansas City, and on the train journey thought up the character that was to change everything – Mickey Mouse. The rest, as they say, is history. Mickey became a national craze and brought in badly needed income. Walt worked so hard that he had a nervous breakdown, but Roy stayed with him and together they built up Walt Disney Productions, a company that went on to make many great films. Walt also created Disneyland and, towards the end of his life, Florida's famous Disney World.

His story underlines several points made in this book: a humble background is no barrier to success; a really determined man is not put off by initial failures; and it pays to give one's imagination free rein. Disney had the courage and vision to try bold new ideas, often against the advice of his colleagues and financial backers (he frequently staked everything on his next project), and he knew how to bring out the best in other creative people. He was fortunate to have the help of a capable brother, but it was his talent and sunny optimism that made the company what it was. He said in his later years:

I have always been bored with just making money. I've wanted to *do* things, I wanted to build things. Get something *going*. People look at me in different ways. Some say, 'the guy has no regard for money'. That is not true. I *have* had regard for money. But I'm not like some people who worship money as something you've got to have piled up in a big pile somewhere. I've only thought of money in one way, and that is to do something with it, you see? I don't think there is a thing that I own that I will ever get the benefit of, except through doing things with it.

Sometimes, of course, the sceptics turn out to be right. Ideas that look brilliant on paper may prove unworkable or too limited in their appeal. But all too often they are rejected for reasons that have nothing to do with their merits. Many people dislike change. They prefer to defend their existing business. Ironically, some of the strongest resistance tends to come from people who have played a major role in previous changes. They not only resent the suggestion that there might be a better way, but have a vested interest in protecting the status quo.

If one works for a large and apparently solid corporation it is all too easy to assume that tomorrow will be more or less like today – that significant change is unlikely, unpredictable, and in any case will come slowly. But tomorrow may not be like today; indeed, it is more realistic to assume that it won't be. We live in what has been aptly described as 'the age of discontinuity'. Entrepreneurs are constantly looking not only for new products but also for new ways of doing things – in manufacturing, in finance, in services, in management, in the arts, in economics. Change is risky, but it may be even more risky not to change.

Henry Ford was one of the business leaders who acknowledged this way back in the 1920s. In *My Life and Work*, he wrote:

If to petrify is success, all one has to do is to humour the lazy side of the mind; but if to grow is success, then one must wake up anew each morning and keep awake all day. I saw great businesses become but a ghost of a name because someone thought they could be managed just as the way they were always managed, and though the management may have been the most excellent in its day, its excellence consisted in its alertness to its day, and not in slavish following of its yesterdays. Life, as I see it, is not a location but a journey. Even the man who feels himself settled is not settled – he is probably sagging back. Everything is in flux, and was meant to be. We may live at the same number of the street but it is never the same man who lives there.

In recent decades, great fortunes have been made in the technology sector. As a result, it has become commonplace to associate the word 'innovation' with technological change. This is a rather narrow interpretation, but the careers of people like Bill Gates and Steve Jobs have certainly been just as remarkable as those of an earlier generation of innovators.

THE VISIONARY

At a London conference in October 2005, a smartly dressed middle-aged American dazzled the audience with his vision of the future.

Before the end of this decade, he said, we will all be carrying information on tablet computers which can be held like a clipboard, with a flat screen on the front. They will be hooked up to the internet and provide our entertainment, education and information needs. The internet will not have speed restrictions and the new devices will be a lot cheaper than the ones we use today. Newspapers, magazines, forms, and textbooks will become redundant in their present form, with interactive, personalised content delivered to the handheld computers. The software in mobile phones will become hugely more sophisticated. Television, too, will be very different. Viewers will be able to personalise everything from news coverage to football.

His listeners paid close attention because the American was not just another scientist or management guru, but a highly successful innovator – Bill Gates.

The story of how he turned a tiny firm into a giant corporation has become part of entrepreneurial folklore and a source of inspiration for thousands of ambitious young men and women. Bill was just nineteen when, in 1975, he and a friend, Paul Allen, registered a partnership in Albuquerque, New Mexico, which they called Microsoft. Both had been 'fooling around' with computers at school but at the time they were huge, cumbersome, and expensive. Bill later enrolled at Harvard with the intention of getting a degree in economics. He also wanted to go into politics.

All this changed when, one day, Paul showed him a magazine, *Popular Electronics*, which had on its cover a photograph of a very small computer. It was being sold as a kit but lacked software – the instructions that tell computers what to do. It couldn't be programmed, which made it more of a novelty than a tool. What it did have, however, was an Intel microprocessor chip as its brain.

'When we saw that', he recalls in his book *The Road Ahead*, 'panic set in. Oh no! It's happening without us! People are going to write real software for this chip.' He was sure that it would happen sooner rather than later and he wanted to be in at the beginning. So he dropped out of Harvard and went into business with Paul, who had been working for Honeywell.

Their first project was to create a programming language,

BASIC, for the little machine. The goal was to get companies like Radio Shack to include their software with the personal computers they sold, and pay them a royalty. The strategy worked: BASIC was soon being used by most manufacturers, including Apple and companies in Japan.

In 1979, they moved Microsoft from Albuquerque to a suburb of their hometown, Seattle. Bill also wanted help with running the business and offered part ownership to an old Harvard pal, Steve Ballmer, who became 'assistant to the President', even though there were only 30 employees.

A significant break came the following year. The leading hardware company, IBM, had been slow to recognise the mass-market potential of personal computers but now wanted to produce a new one in less than a year. The management decided that, in order to meet such a tight schedule, it had to involve outsiders. It would buy the microprocessors from Intel and lease the operating system from Microsoft. Bill eagerly accepted the challenge. He and his team devised what became known as the Microsoft Disk Operating System, or MS-DOS. They granted IBM the right to use it on as many computers as it could sell, in return for a low one-time fee. The aim was to profit from licensing MS-DOS to companies that wanted to offer machines more or less compatible with the new IBM computer. IBM could use their software for free, but it did not have an exclusive license or control of future enhancements.

It was a shrewd deal. The computer hit the market in August 1981 and became the hardware standard; by the mid-1980s there were dozens of models of IBM-compatible PCs.

Bill and his team thought long and hard about their next step. In 1983, he announced that Microsoft was planning to bring graphical computing to the IBM PC, with a product called Windows. He worked closely with Apple on the development of a new computer, the Macintosh. Everything about the Macintosh's operating system was graphical and it was a huge success.

The business relationship with IBM remained vital to Microsoft. In 1986, Bill took the company public – his stake made him a billionaire at 30. He proposed to IBM that they buy 30 per cent of the shares but they weren't interested. They also turned down his offer to develop a new system and license it to IBM; the management wanted to be involved in the creation of any software it considered to be strategic. He pressed on with Windows, which continued to evolve. Today there are more than a billion computers in the world and 90 per cent of these are dependent on Microsoft technology. Bill has become enormously rich. So have members of his team: Steve Ballmer, now the company's chief executive, is reckoned to have a net worth of more than $13 billion. But Bill insists that he is not interested in money for its own sake. 'What's important', he says, 'is to keep moving ahead, keep changing, keep fresh'. He has increasingly turned to philanthropic efforts through the Bill & Melinda Gates Foundation and says that he will give away 95 per cent of his wealth before his death. He has, however, built a huge and extravagant house on the shores of Lake Washington. It has a movie theatre, a pool, a sport court and all the latest electronic gadgets.

Critics have accused Microsoft of monopolistic behaviour, but the company faces many challenges in an ever-changing industry. It dominates the operating software 'platform', but the new platform is the internet, and on that front it's up against formidable competition such as Google.

'Success', Bill told a *Sunday Times* interviewer in 1995, 'is a lousy teacher – it seduces smart people into thinking that they can't lose'. Although he is no longer involved in day-to-day management, he plainly does not intend to be one of them. As his conference speech showed, he still has lots of ideas, and Microsoft has the financial clout to turn many of them into reality.

INSANELY GREAT

Another visionary played a major role in the early days of the personal computer – Steve Jobs. His story is even more remarkable than that of Gates. The company he co-founded, Apple Computer, drove him away but years later he made a dramatic comeback. He also became a significant force in the entertainment industry.

Steve was born on 24 February 1955, in San Francisco. His mother decided to give him up for adoption, and within weeks of his birth she signed over legal custody of her infant son to a local couple, Paul and Clara Jobs. He only found out that they were not his natural parents when he was grown and famous.

Steve was, by all accounts, a difficult child – mischievous and wilful. He found school boring and his assignments a waste of time. He was more interested in electronics and, like Bill Gates, later dropped out of college.

One day a friend introduced him to an older boy, Steven Wozniak, who had built a rudimentary computer in his garage. Jobs was intrigued by the project but went to work for Atari, a company that was making popular video games. They gave him some minor tasks and when he said that he wanted to go to India (seeking spiritual enlightenment had become fashionable among young Americans) they raised no objections. He returned some months later, wearing saffron robes and sporting a shaved head. Most other employers would have been appalled but hey, this was Silicon Valley, and he got his job back. But he also wanted to find out what Wozniak had been up to, and went to see him in his garage.

'Woz', as everyone called him, had been working for

Hewlett-Packard, but the pair became friends and eventually decided to set up their own business. In April 1976, Woz and Jobs signed a document that gave them equal shares in Apple Computer. They had very little capital and found it hard to raise more. It also emerged that retailers wanted real computers, not just the circuit board that Woz had designed.

By the summer of that year they had a working mock-up of a machine which they took to the first Personal Computer Festival in Atlantic City. Retailers said they found it interesting but made it clear that, if Apple wanted to make an impact, the product had to be a complete, self-contained computer that would satisfy their customers. Woz went back to the garage where the fledging company had based its operation and worked hard on developing the right kind of machine. The other Steve kept up his efforts to find an investor. He got lucky: a former executive from Intel who had become wealthy agreed to back them in return for part ownership of the business, which became a corporation.

Their new computer, Apple II, was unveiled at a trade show on the West Coast in 1977. It made a favourable impression and orders poured in. By 1978 the corporation had 60 employees. Jobs was the driving force (he liked slogans like 'Insanely great!') but he wasn't an easy man to work with. Abrasive and impatient, he was always striving for perfection. Apple II was good, but they could do better. The machine was upgraded and released as Apple III, but he also had another project in mind – a computer he named Lisa. It went ahead but took longer, and cost more, than expected. The board decided to put someone else in charge of new product development. To soften the blow, he was made Chairman. They wanted to make a public stock offering and thought that he could generate useful publicity.

When the initial public offering (IPO) took place in December 1980 it was a huge success. Overnight, Steve Jobs was worth more than $217 million, making him one of the richest self-made men in America at the age of 25.

But he still wanted to be involved at the sharp end. An experimental machine called the Mackintosh caught his eye and he set up a small team in a separate building. The board let him get on with it but the old problems arose. He still wanted to run the company but the board appointed an outsider, John Scully, as President. The Apple III and the Lisa had flopped and Steve's projections for the Mackintosh also seemed unrealistic. The Mac was finally released in January 1984. Early sales reports were encouraging, but the euphoria didn't last. The company had a serious problem and Scully decided to strip him of any operating role in Apple. Steve's response was that he would start a new venture of his own. He explained his reasons in an interview with *Newsweek*.

I personally, man, want to build things. I'm 30. I'm not ready to be an industry pundit. I got three offers to be a professor during the summer, and I told all of the universities that I thought I would be an awful professor.

What I'm best at doing is finding a group of talented people and making things with them. I respect the direction that Apple is going in. But for me personally, you know, I want to make things. And if there's no place for me to make things there, then I'll do what I did twice before. I'll make my own place. You know I did it in the garage when Apple started, and I did it in the metaphorical garage when the Mac started.

I helped shepherd Apple from a garage to a billion-and-a-half-dollar company. It took a bunch of rambunctious upstarts, working with very little resources and a certain vision and commitment, to do it. I'm probably not the best person in the world to shepherd it to a five- or ten-billion-dollar company, which I think is probably its destiny. And so I haven't got any sort of odd chip on my shoulder about proving anything to myself or anybody else. I had ten of the best years of my life, you know, and I don't regret much of anything. I want to get on with my life.

A scientist at Stanford University convinced him that there was scope for a new type of computer specifically tailored to the educational market. This became his new project. He resigned as chairman of Apple, sold his stock, and launched a company he named NeXT.

The new computer, housed in a cube, was released in 1989 but made little headway in the market. Steve also had problems with another venture – a business he had bought from George Lucas, the creator of *Star Wars*, for $10 million. Called Pixar, it specialised in computer graphics and had developed a machine, the Pixar Image Computer. He thought it would sell to the medical community but there was no real demand for it.

The future looked bleak. He had invested much of his fortune and must have been tempted to give up, but he wasn't too proud to admit that he had failed again. Two things saved him. He shut down the NeXT hardware business and concentrated on software, and he did a deal with Disney under which Pixar would produce computer-animated movies.

Meanwhile, Apple had also gone from bad to worse. Scully had been forced out in 1993 and his successor decided to sell the company. But negotiations with a potential buyer got nowhere. Steve asked for a meeting with the board and said that they needed a new CEO: he, as the co-founder, was the obvious choice. They didn't agree but eventually decided that he was right. They also bought NeXT for $377 million in cash and $1.5 million in Apple shares. Steve was back with a vengeance.

He got most of the board to resign within weeks and made drastic changes, which got Apple back on track. It went on to produce highly successful products like the iPod, the iMac, and the Power Mac. He also continued to run Pixar and in November 1995 floated the company on the stock market. It made him a billionaire.

But there was another shock in the making. In 2004, he was told that he had pancreatic cancer and had no more than six months left to live. By sheer good luck, he was spared: doctors found that he had a very rare form of the disease that was treatable by surgery.

In a speech to students at Stanford University the following year, he explained what drives his decision-making. 'Remembering that I'll be dead soon', he said, 'is the most important tool I have ever encountered to help me make the big choices in life. Because almost everything – all external expectations, all pride, all fear of embarrassment or failure – these things just fall away in the face of death, leaving only what is truly important. Remembering that you are going to die is the best way I know to avoid the trap of thinking that you have something to lose. You are already naked. There is no reason not to follow your heart.'

Early in 2006, Disney announced that it was buying Pixar, which had made blockbusters like *Toy Story* and *Finding Nemo*, for $7.4 billion in stock. Jobs, who still owned half the business, became the biggest individual shareholder in Disney and a powerful player in Hollywood. He joined the board, but associates say that his heart remains with Apple.

One of the most talented members of his team, Jonathan Ive, is from Chigwell in Essex. The son of a silversmith, he went to college in Gateshead and later co-founded a small independent design consultancy in London. Apple was one of the clients and offered him a job. He crossed the Atlantic, but this was at the time when the company was in trouble and none of his designs were implemented. Everything changed when Steve Jobs returned and asked him to start work on a new computer, which became the hugely successful iMac.

Jonathan has since been closely involved in the creation of other winners, such as the iPod. His official title is senior vice-president in charge of industrial design, but unofficially he has been called 'Steve's corporate son'. Like his boss, he likes to dress in black t-shirt and sneakers; all that is missing is a place in the billionaire's club.

NET PLAYERS

The internet boom of the late 1990s made fortunes for many other entrepreneurs, at least on paper. All they needed was a plausible idea for a website, a catchy name for their start-up, and contacts in the financial community who could find venture capital or arrange an IPO. Investors rushed in because they, too, expected to make easy money.

The people who handled the flotations usually mentioned that there were 'risk factors'. The prospectus would point out that the company had a new and unproven business 'model' and that the share price was expected to be 'highly volatile'. It would also stress that 'there can be no assurance that it will ever achieve or sustain profitability or that the operating losses will not increase in future'.

Many investors came to regret that they failed to heed the warning, but such was the speculative frenzy at the time that it made little difference. The internet was going to change the world, and the start-ups could not be judged by the normal criteria.

It was an argument I had heard during previous stock market bubbles. They had ended in tears and I thought it was likely to happen again. When I said so in the *Evening Standard* I was accused of being a 'dinosaur'. We could all get rich!

The mood changed when financial institutions and other investors began to take a more realistic view. Many start-ups had spent a lot of money on advertising their brand and had little to show for it. IPOs became more difficult and venture capitalists were reluctant to put up more cash. A growing number of companies went bust or merged with others.

The basic problem with the first version of the internet was that it was long on vision but short on execution and the audience. When the boom got under way, the internet had been in existence for only a few years. It was the outgrowth of a US government network, the Aparnet, which initially had been used solely for computer-science and engineering projects. The internet came into being as a commercial service when the government decided in 1989 to stop funding the Aparnet.

The first online companies tiptoed onto the scene in the early 1990s. They made little impact, but one, Netscape, created a stir when it went public in 1995. The success of the flotation encouraged others to have a go. But the technology was still rudimentary and the business models were based on guesswork. No one *knew* if there was a big market out there and, if there was, how profitable the ventures might be.

The web has since become a platform, and building new businesses on that platform is a less expensive proposition. Start-ups are leveraging a decade's worth of work on technologies that are now proven. More people are online than ever before and the companies that survived the bust (or later entrants) should be able to enjoy many years of growth. The internet has become exciting again.

A key factor has been the vast improvement in search engines. It has made fortunes for young men like Larry Page and the Russian-born Sergey Brin, who met as Stanford University graduate students in 1995 and later launched Google. (The name is a play on the word 'googol', which is the mathematical term for the numeral 1 followed by 100 zeros. Their name reflects the company's mission to organise the immense, seemingly infinite amount of information available on the web 'just for you'.)

Page and Brin entered the market after other major search players, but their answers were seen by people as more accurate and relevant to what they were looking for. They managed to get venture capital funding, but there was little interest in licensing deals. The breakthrough came with the realisation that they could build a targeted advertising model that would show you ads that are relevant to you when you searched for a specific topic, and then charge advertisers for the number of times that users clicked on their ads. Google know exactly what you are interested in – after all, you are searching for it – and can link you up with advertisers directly or indirectly connected to your searches.

By the middle of 2000, Google was handling 15 million searches a day and doing well financially. In 2004, the company was floated on the stock market at $80 a share. It continued to grow: in 2005, the business had $6 billion in revenues and, more impressively, was so profitable that it generated almost half as much cash as Time Warner, the global media conglomerate. Wall Street analysts calculated that it was ten times more valuable than General Motors.

Google now processes roughly a billion searches a day. Only a third are US-based, and less than half are in English – it is searchable in 100 languages. *Forbes* magazine reckons that each of the founders, who are still in their early 30s, have a net worth of almost $13 billion. But they are well aware that there will be new challengers and that the company must continue to innovate if it wants to stay ahead.

Another company that has become world famous is Amazon, the online retailer founded in 1995 by Jeff Bezos. A graduate of Princeton University (computer science and electrical engineering), he became interested in the worldwide web while working for a hedge fund on Wall Street. At the time, there was no e-commerce to speak of, but Jeff thought it had great potential. He quit his well-paid job and at the age of 31 embarked on the venture that would make him a billionaire.

The story has often been told how he and his wife went to Seattle; she drove, he typed the business plan on a laptop. Like Bill Gates and Steve Jobs, he started the company in a garage. It was originally incorporated as Cadabra (as in Abracadabra). But Jeff changed the name to Amazon because the original sounded too much like 'cadaver'. A contact had told him that annual book sales in the US were about $65 billion and he decided to target that market. People said he was crazy, and he found it hard to get financial backing – it took months, and many meetings, to raise a million dollars from 22 different angle investors.

There was a point in 1995 when Amazon very easily might not have continued to exist, but Jeff was determined to press on. He believes that optimism is an essential quality for doing anything hard. That doesn't mean one is blind or unrealistic; it means that you keep focused on eliminating risks and modifying your strategy until it is a strategy about which you can be *genuinely* optimistic.

Jeff says that Amazon has got much bigger, and much faster, than he had predicted. The business has grown from books to products in 35 categories and serves more than 45 million customers. Critics say he was wrong to stress growth above profitability, but he insists that it made sense:

> We have always tried to be very clear with people that we are an appropriate company only for long-term investors. I think there will be more change and opportunity in the next ten years than over the last ten. We

can build more shareholder value by lowering product prices than we can by trying to raise margins. It's a more patient approach but I believe that it leads to a stronger, healthier company. It also serves customers much, much better. We are dedicated to the notion of, year in and year out, lowering prices and getting more efficient so that we can afford to do that.

Jeff has certainly done well himself: *Forbes* puts his net worth at $4.4 billion. He says that he buys about ten books a month, and reads three, and that he is a big fan of science fiction. Still in his early 40s, he is an extrovert with a keen sense of humour (the late Peter Sellers is one of his heroes) and undiminished optimism. He once told an interviewer: 'My wife says that if Jeff is unhappy, wait three minutes.'

THE SHOPKEEPER

If the net players are right, traditional retailers should be worried about their future. Rapid growth in online sales means that the internet has become a serious threat to shopping malls, department stores and high streets. Most retailers have responded by making the development of internet activities part of their overall business strategy, but the tough question is how much emphasis they should put on it. Does it make sense to go on investing in expensive space and employing shop assistants?

As behaviourists keep pointing out, we are social animals. Online shopping is convenient, and the ease with which we can compare prices is an important factor, but we don't want to live like hermits. We still go to the cinema and the theatre, even though we can get a cornucopia of entertainment at home, and we continue to shop in stores and boutiques because it's an enjoyable social experience.

Britain's top shopkeeper, Sir Philip Green, remains optimistic. He has built up a sprawling empire of 2,500 shops, including the Bhs chain, and has twice tried to buy Marks & Spencer. (He failed, but wouldn't have attempted to do so if he thought that the days of the high street were numbered.)

Green is another entrepreneur whose story has inspired many ambitious young people. He left school at sixteen without a single O level, and after working as an apprentice for a wholesale footwear company set up his own business in London's rag trade, buying and selling clothes imported from Hong Kong. His start-up capital was just £9,500 – money raised by means of a short-term bank loan. The venture flopped but he is not the kind of man who gives up at the first hurdle. In 1981, he bought a shop lease in New Bond Street and sold designer clothes at discount prices, a move that made him enemies and did not produce the profits he had hoped for.

His break came when he was able to buy a struggling company, called Jean Jeanie, for £65,000. It had 60 shops and was one of the country's biggest denim-retailers, but it also had an overdraft of more than £3 million. Convinced that he could turn the company around, he promised to repay it within six months. He did well enough to attract the attention of Lee Cooper Jeans, which offered to buy him out if he agreed to become managing director of its new retail division. They eventually settled on a price of £7 million. The deal not only enabled him to repay the loan but also made him a millionaire.

Like so many other entrepreneurs, however, he found it difficult to work for someone else and he resigned before the end of his contract.

The following year a new opportunity arose: the prospect of a bid to rescue a publicly quoted fashion company called Amber Day. He managed to raise the necessary capital, and became Chairman and chief executive, with a personal 17 per cent holding. It turned out to be another unhappy experience. The City did not like his autocratic style and he was forced to quit. He collected a pay-off of £1.1 million and made £7.6 million from selling his shares, which enabled him to buy a fashion chain that had gone into receivership. When the deal was struck, he announced that the company now belonged to him and his family: 'That's the way it is and that's the way it'll stay.'

Green went on to make other acquisitions. One of his boldest moves was a bid for the Sears empire put together in the 1950s and 60s by Charles Clore. He was able to get help from bankers and friends like the secretive Barclay brothers, who put £100 million into a new take-over vehicle, January Investments, and he succeeded in gaining control. He promptly dismantled Sears. The take-over team had paid £548 million for the group and he sold the parts for around £800 million, thus pocketing £250 million in profit.

Cash-rich, he next decided to go after Marks & Spencer. It was a very different proposition – buying it would cost more than £10 billion. The board mounted a vigorous defence and he eventually pulled out. He turned, instead, to British Home Stores. It was owned by Storehouse and they were eager to sell; he got the company for £250 million. Green held 94 per cent of the equity and he took it private. He and allies like Richard Caring, a major supplier of Third World clothes, transformed the business, now known as Bhs. Profits soared and by 2002 he was a billionaire, at least on paper.

He next tried to buy Woolworths but the talks collapsed. He then went after Arcadia, the parent company of Topshop, Dorothy Perkins, Miss Selfridge, Wallis, and Burton. His offer of £690 million was rejected by the board but it gave in when he raised it. He ended up with 92 per cent of shares and Arcadia, too, became a private company. Green proudly told the *Financial Times*: 'Look back in history at all the great entrepreneurs. People talk about those like Hanson as great empire builders. But that was all done through stock market money. I have done this as a solo artist.'

It was a formidable achievement, but he still wanted the biggest prize of all – Marks & Spencer – and decided to have another go. He assembled an impressive group of financial backers and said he would commit up to £1 billion of his money. The board opposed him, as it had done before, and a hard-fought battle ended in the same way: he withdrew.

Green and his wife, Tina, are said to have accumulated a fortune of nearly £5 billion, making them one of the richest couples in Britain. The figure is based, to a large extent, on what Bhs and Arcadia are reckoned to be worth. The media still calls Green 'the king of the high street', but he is well aware that the value of the businesses is by no means fixed. As he has so often shown, it ultimately depends on what someone is willing to pay for them. He is more likely to be a buyer than a seller, but a dramatic change in shopping habits would certainly influence his judgement.

Meantime, the couple pay themselves handsome dividends and have built up a substantial portfolio of other assets. The bulk of their wealth is in Tina's name, for tax reasons. Born in London, the daughter of wine merchants, she grew up in Japan and Hong Kong. In 1998 she moved to Monaco with their children, Chloe and Brandon. Philip commutes weekly to London in their Gulfstream jet. They have a luxury yacht, and love to give parties, but Tina is also involved in the business – she designed the Home Store concept at their flagship store in Chichester, and Philip says that he trusts his wife utterly in matters of interior decoration. 'It's not a hobby', she told reporters at the launch of the new concept. 'I live it, I breathe it. I love everything about designing a home. This is my baby.'

THE PORN BARONS

The internet has already hit another part of the retail trade –
the market for top-shelf magazines. Soft porn has long been
a lucrative business, but sales have declined because there
are now so many websites that offer sexual titillation.

Playboy, the world's best-known title, has responded by
introducing an online edition, as well as an 'adult' TV
channel. Christie Hefner, who runs her father Hugh Hefner's
company, says that she intends to create a multimedia, multi-
platform enterprise.

Hef, as he likes to be called, created the magazine in the
1950s with $600 of borrowed money. It was an instant success
and, ever since, has enabled him to have the kind of lifestyle
his readers aspire to – a mansion in Beverly Hills, fawning
acolytes, endless parties, and a succession of gorgeous play-
mates. He still had three young girlfriends living with him
when he celebrated his 80th birthday in April 2006. 'I consider
myself the luckiest cat on the planet', he told the *Independent*.

Christie once suggested that I should edit a new magazine
he wanted to launch in Europe. I could, she thought, be the
'new Hef'. I told her that, although I shared his *joie de vivre*, I
couldn't see myself as a pipe-smoking Lothario in silk pyjamas
hell-bent on sleeping with as many women as possible and
telling the world about my conquests.

One of the British pioneers in the top-shelf trade was Paul
Raymond, who has used his profits to buy property in Soho
and is reckoned to have assets of £600 million. Another was
David Sullivan, a flashy 'Essex boy' who now owns Sport
Newspapers and the biggest chain of licensed sex shops in
the country. He is in partnership with David Gold, a former
bricklayer who became a girlie-mag mogul in the 1960s and
bought the Ann Summers shops in 1972. Said to be worth
more than £500 million, he has a mansion in Surrey with a

55-acre garden and golf course. He also owns a helicopter and a fleet of planes which he charters out as Gold Air.

Richard Desmond, the proprietor of Express Newspapers and *OK* magazine, is another entrepreneur who made his first fortune in the porn business. He left school at fifteen and tried his hand at various jobs, including jazz drummer and ad salesman, before getting into the trade. He fared so well that he was able to buy Express Newspapers for £125 million in 2000. Richard has sold off the girlie mags (including titles like *Asian Babes* and *Readers' Wives*), and rails against people who call him a pornographer, but he has kept his adult television channels. He says that he makes a million a week, and his personal wealth is estimated at £1.9 billion in the *Sunday Times* rich list, but like his friend Philip Green he is a workaholic who still puts in long hours at the office.

THE MAVERICK

We all know Richard Branson, or think we do. He is the bearded entrepreneur who, it seems, will do anything to gain publicity for his various enterprises. He has dressed up as a can of Virgin Cola, donned a wedding dress to launch a bridal fashion venture, posed with a Virgin mobile phone as a codpiece, and flown around the world in a hot-air balloon.

Branson is a global superstar of self-aggrandisement. The media loves his stunts; the serious chaps in City boardrooms say that it's all rather juvenile. The public admires him because of his David against Goliath stance in taking on traditional interests and doesn't begrudge him his wealth, which they see as earned by his own efforts. In America, he is often portrayed as a British eccentric. But there is method in his apparent madness. His antics have created hugely valuable brand awareness and have made him super-rich. They disguise what financial institutions have come to understand – that Branson is a shrewd businessman, a maverick who backs his hunches, takes great risks, and has an enviable flair for making lucrative deals.

Like many other financial journalists, I used to think that his bold gambles would end in tears. This was also the view taken by many people in the City; they worried about his impetuosity and the mystery that cloaked his operations. During the 1990s, many of us repeatedly sought to answer the question: 'Is Branson going bust?' If that was ever a serious risk, it is no longer. One of his most impressive deals was the sale, early in 2006, of Virgin Mobile for £962 million, scarcely six years after it was launched. His original investment was about £45 million.

Richard Charles Nicholas Branson is a Londoner, born in 1950. The menfolk in his family had been lawyers for several generations. His mother had been a dancer and, later, an air hostess in South America – at a time when you had to wear an oxygen mask to fly over mountains. They lived in Guildford, Surrey, but Richard was sent away to boarding school at the age of eight. He says that he was 'pretty hopeless' in the class-room but eventually managed to gain admission to Stowe, one of Britain's prestigious public schools. While there, he and a friend made plans to start a magazine called *Student*. He spent a great deal of time soliciting ads for the first issue and writing letters to names in *Who's Who* asking for editorial contributions. Then, with £3,000 of ad revenue in hand, he left Stowe at the age of seventeen to work full time on the project. *Student* was launched in January 1968 but never made money and did not last long. He says that the experience taught him more than he could ever have learned at school or university.

Richard next decided to sell records by mail order. He called his new venture Virgin, which he later said was an acknowledgement of his naivety in business. Whatever the reason, it was an eye-catching name which he has used ever since. The enterprise was often short of cash, and when it was threatened by a postal strike he bought a shop in Oxford Street. Other shops followed and he also founded his own Virgin record label, which had a great commercial success with Mike Oldfield's *Tubular Bells.*

What really astonished everyone was his announcement, in 1984, that he would start a new airline. Freddie Laker had gone bust; Branson, who admitted that he knew even less about the industry, would surely meet the same fate. He swept all objections aside. 'If you sit down with accountants and look at profit and loss projections', he said, 'they'll manage to come up with all sorts of reasons why something won't work. Well, I think if you've got a gut feeling about something then trial and error can produce the best results. I think the only way to learn is to give it a try.'

Virgin Atlantic was launched with one jumbo jet. British Airways was dismissive but became concerned when Branson acquired more planes and encroached on its most profitable routes. In 1992, Branson sold Virgin Music to Thorn-EMI for £500 million in order to concentrate all his energies on his airline.

Lord King, the BA chairman, still felt confident that he could see off the challenge from a young man he contemptuously referred to as the 'grinning pullover'. As editor of *High Life,* and one of his friends, I had a ringside seat at the battle that followed. Branson accused BA of running a 'dirty tricks' campaign against Virgin: his most serious allegation was that it had sought to discredit him by spreading false information and rumours in the press. I thought that he greatly exaggerated the damage done by whatever some of the BA staff had got up to, but in the end King was forced to apologise. The grinning pullover had won a famous victory and made the most of it. What really mattered, though, was that Virgin had established a strong base for further growth. In 1999, Branson persuaded Singapore Airlines to hand over £600 million for 49 per cent of the company, which has since become a leading player in the industry.

I have met Richard on a number of occasions and have always been struck by the contrast between his public personality and his private behaviour. Face to face, he tends to be rather shy and awkward. He stutters and at times is almost apologetic. At a small informal dinner I hosted during my years as Chairman of the British Tourist Authority, he barely said a word. Others have had the same experience. It helps to explain, I think, why so many people have made the mistake of underestimating one of the most successful entrepreneurs of his generation.

EASY WAYS

Richard's concept of 'stretching the brand' has been adopted by another entrepreneur who is seldom out of the headlines and who readily admits that he had been inspired by him.

Stelios Haji-Ioannou came to the attention of the British public when, like Richard, he decided to launch an airline. He was 28 when he created easyJet – now one of the largest short-haul carriers in Europe. He is so fond of the word 'easy', that he has used it for a wide range of other ventures – internet cafés, cinemas, car hire, pizza delivery, hotels, personal finance and cruises.

Stelios (he prefers to use his first name, which is certainly easier for most of us) was born in Greece on 14 February 1967. His father was a shipping magnate and he went to high school in Athens before coming to Britain to study at the London School of Economics. He also graduated from the City of London University Business School with an MSc in Shipping Trade and Economics.

Not surprisingly, his first business venture, at the age of 25, was in the industry he knew so well. This was before he got hooked on easy ways, so it was called Stelmar Shipping. He has since sold it for £470 million. His family still owns a large stake in easyJet, but he sees himself more as a brand manager than as chief executive of one of the group's companies. Asked by the *New York Times* how his ideas originate, he said:

> It is a lot trial and error, and using my personal experience from other industries. With the cruise line, I came up with the idea of staying in port at night from my personal experience and memories of private yachting. I grew up being on boats because my father had a yacht. What do you do with a yacht? You sail during the day and go into port at night, which is not the itinerary of traditional cruises. Cruising in the middle of the night is not pleasant. You look out at a dark sea. Sailing during daylight and arriving in the afternoon is better. You actually see views.

Critics have accused him of being obsessed with the colour orange. His response is that: 'We want to be faithful to the brand, and the colour is part of that. It tells people that we are about value for money and fun.'

Stelios can afford to experiment: with property and other assets, his family is reputed to be worth more than £700 million. Still only 39, and recently knighted, he runs his business from a no-frills office in London and plainly does not intend to take it easy – there is so much that he still wants to do. His tip for success: 'Always try to make it balanced. Say: this is the upside, but it could go wrong because of this, and that's how I plan to deal with the risk.'

CHAPTER 4

BETTER RICH THAN RED

When the Soviet Union collapsed in 1991, few people outside
the bleak industrialised town of Ukhta, in the far north of
Russia, had heard of a young man called Roman Abramovich.
There was no reason why they should have done so. He was
just another small-time entrepreneur who had used his wife's
dowry to engage in black-market trading of perfume, deodor-
ants, tights, and toothpaste that were much in demand during
the communist era. It was a risky game – one false move and
he would have been arrested by the KGB. The reforms
introduced by Mikhail Gorbachev offered more room for
manoeuvre. The couple set up a business venture in their tiny
flat, selling plastic ducks. It gave them a better standard of
living but did not make them rich.

All this changed when Boris Yeltsin became president of
Russia. He is now remembered mainly because of his brave
stand against Marxist plotters, and his obvious fondness for
vodka, but he was also responsible for the chaotic privatisation
of state-owned assets in the mid-1990s. They included an oil
company, Sibneft.

By then, Abramovich had become involved in the lucrative

oil business, initially on a small scale. He eventually teamed up with a wealthy tycoon, Boris Berezovsky, and along with others they snapped up the ridiculously under-priced Sibneft. They were not the only people who benefited from Yeltsin's foolishness: what was billed as free-market economics was in fact a quick-fire sale of Russia's wealth to Kremlin cronies.

One of the leading oligarchs, as they were known, was Mikhail Khodorkovsky, a former communist youth activist who founded the Yukos oil company. He became the country's richest man, with an estimated fortune of $15 billion, but his luck ran out when Vladimir Putin took over from Yeltsin. He was arrested and charged with tax evasion and fraud. Khodorkovsky protested that the charges were trumped up by the Kremlin to punish him for challenging its energy policy and funding opposition parties. But his company was forcibly renationalised and he was sentenced to eight years in prison after a trial that was widely seen as a sham. He ended up in a penal colony near the Russian border with China and Mongolia. 'The Kremlin has tried to isolate me completely from people and the country, and to destroy me physically', he said in a statement. 'They hope that I will soon be forgotten. They are trying to convince you, friends, that the fight is over. That you must resign yourself to domination by a self-serving bureaucracy in Russia. This is not true. The fight is only just beginning.'

Bold talk, but there was little public sympathy for him. The oligarchs were seen as greedy opportunists who got rich at the expense of their fellow citizens.

Before his downfall, Khodorkovsky, the 42-year-old father of three, had lived in a villa in Moscow and was ferried around in an armoured limousine or private jet. His new home was, and still is, a bunkbed in one of thirteen dormitory blocks. Winter temperatures drop to −40°C and the colony is riddled with tuberculosis. His Italian suits have been swapped for dark blue prison fatigues and, like other prisoners, he has to rise daily at 6 am for various chores – cleaning, bread-baking and mending equipment. Many Russians feel that he deserves his harsh punishment.

Boris Berezovsky would almost certainly have suffered the same fate if he had stayed in Russia when his relationship with the Kremlin soured in 2000. Granted political asylum in Britain, he now runs his affairs from an office in Mayfair.

Roman Abramovich, his former business partner, played his cards differently. He made a pact with Putin to stay out of national politics and did not resist his attempts to re-establish state control of the oil industry. He also responded to the president's call for oligarchs to be more socially responsible. He became governor of Chukotka, a remote and impoverished region in the far east of Russia and invested more than $1 billion in schools, hospitals, apartment blocks and other infrastructure. When his term expired in 2005, Putin asked him to serve for another five years. He agreed, even though he was spending more and more time abroad.

Abramovich first came to the attention of the British public in 2003 when he bought Chelsea FC for £140 million. It was a surprising move – why, people asked, did a Russian billionaire want to own an *English* club? His advisers explained that he had fallen in love with football after going to a Champions League quarter-final of Manchester United vs. Real Madrid, and had asked them to find out what clubs in England might be available. They came up with five, including Manchester United, Spurs, and Chelsea. He chose Chelsea because it was in serious financial trouble and eager to do a deal. Many fans, unaware that their club had sunk into a quagmire of debt, objected to the arrival of this upstart foreigner but changed their mind when he spent many more millions in a determined effort to reverse years of underachievement. In the long term', he told them, 'our strategy is to build the most successful football club in the world'. The Russian media, understandably, said that it would have been more patriotic to back one of the teams in his homeland.

The mayor of Moscow said that it was tantamount to 'spitting at Russia'. Abramovich has since set up a national academy to train footballers and finance coaches. He has paid for 50 pitches across the country and is building a £60-million football stadium in Moscow. Due to be completed by 2008, it will hold 50,000 spectators and have an automated glass roof. He is also reported to have discussed plans for a Formula One circuit with the Mayor.

His investment has been welcomed by Putin, a judo black-belt and football fan, who has often called for sport to play a greater role in the life of ordinary Russians. Abramovich can well afford it. In 2005, he sealed one of the biggest business deals in Russia's history when Gazprom, the state gas giant, signed an agreement to pay $13 billion for a 72.7 per cent stake in Sibneft held by Millhouse Capital, the company through which Abramovich controls his empire. The media-shy tycoon has not revealed precisely how much of Millhouse he owns, but industry insiders estimated that he ended up with a cash payment of around $9 billion. It was an extra-ordinary windfall for a man born into poverty and orphaned at the age of four, who used to sell plastic toys.

The wife who helped with that early venture is no longer with him. The couple divorced before he got rich, and she married a musician. When the *Daily Mail* sent a reporter to interview her at their Moscow flat, she told him that she had heard about the deal with no regret. 'The money is too much to comprehend', she said, 'but I doubt that it can bring happiness'.

Perhaps not, but it enables him to live in luxury. Soon after their divorce he met a blonde Aeroflot hostess, Irina Malandina, who became his next wife and the mother of his five children. They have a townhouse in London, a Sussex estate, a country house outside Moscow, a villa on the Côte d'Azur, several yachts and two jets.

His ostentatious display of wealth has been criticised by the Russian media but Putin doesn't seem to mind as long as he sticks to their pact. It has also made his family a target for criminals, so he employs tough bodyguards.

Abramovich is the best-known billionaire but there are now more than 30 others. They include Roustam Tariko, who made his fortune by turning Russians into debt-laden consumers. Born in a small village in Tatarstan, he never knew his father and was raised by his mother, who worked for the Communist Party. Moscow was a depressing place when he arrived there in 1979, aged seventeen. I can well imagine how he felt, because I visited it myself around the same time.

The corrupt bosses in the Kremlin lived like millionaires. They had large apartments, servants, special clinics, country dachas and chauffeur-driven limos that sped down lanes reserved for their use. They also had their own shops, where they could buy whatever they wanted. Ordinary Muscovites knew all about these perks but there was nothing they could do; everyone was afraid of everybody and everything. Most families lived in drab apartment blocks, often in one room. Few had cars. Food was always in short supply; people stood patiently in long queues, hoping that there would still be bread or vegetables when they finally got into the shop. (It reminded me of George Orwell's dictum: all animals are equal, but some are more equal than others.)

Roustam Tariko took classes to prepare for enrolment at a Moscow college, and cleaned streets in return for a small flat in the centre of town. Like Abramovich, he saw a business opportunity when Mikhail Gorbachev replaced the old guard and began to talk about 'glasnost'. Foreigners were arriving in greater numbers and Tariko focused on selling concierge-like services to them. By 1989, he had a good income. He then started to import Italian chocolates and liquor, and also created a brand of his own: Russian Standard Vodka. When the country went through a financial crisis in the 1990s, he founded Russian Standard Bank, a pioneer in consumer credit that gave millions of people their first chance to buy dishwashers, TVs and fridges. Today the bank is the nation's largest consumer lender and Tariko is reckoned to have a fortune of nearly $2 billion.

Moscow has changed dramatically. It has smart hotels, good restaurants, nightclubs, trendy boutiques and supermarkets. Its outskirts are dotted with dachas once reserved for Communist party leaders but now owned by the newly rich. An entire town is being built for millionaires; it is expected to be twice the size of Monaco.

Many have also bought homes in Britain and in Europe's sunny playgrounds (Tariko has a house in Sardinia). London is said to have more than 200,000 Russian speakers and is often referred to as Londongrad or Moscow-on-Thames. They may not all be super-rich but they have had a considerable impact on property prices and they *love* to shop. (There is a joke doing the rounds of the emigré community. A wealthy businessman is on his deathbed and says to his wife: 'Olga, promise me that you will bury me at Harrods.' Shocked, she begs him to reconsider, pointing out that he is rich enough to rest in a fancy Moscow mausoleum. 'No, no', he interrupts. 'Don't you see? If I'm at Harrods, at least I know that you will visit me once a week.')

Gorbachev, who nowadays goes on lecture tours around the world (Americans pay large sums to hear him speak, because it makes them feel good), says that his successor was wrong to give away so much of Russia's wealth to the oligarchs and allow them to run the country, but insists that he is in favour of a market economy. He expects Putin to renationalise more enterprises, but other republics are heading in a different direction. The President of the Ukraine decided in 2005 to hold a live television auction for his country's largest steel plant. There was real competition, and a final price more than double the starting one. The winner was a foreigner, Lakshmi Mittal ('Britain's richest man'), who paid a hefty $4.8 billion. Khazakhstan, a country with some of the most valuable fossil fuel and mineral resources in the world, has also welcomed foreign investors. Vladimir Kim, a leading entrepreneur, joined the billionaire ranks when he floated his copper company on the London Stock Exchange.

When communism was still seen as the biggest threat to the rich in the West, Americans displayed a bumper sticker that proclaimed 'better dead than red'. In Moscow and other parts of the former Soviet empire, the new slogan is 'better rich than red'.

CHAPTER 5

THE SMART ASIANS

Lakshmi Mittal is the most successful of the many Asians who have made their home in Britain. He is estimated to have a fortune of £15 billion, but is on record as saying that he 'never felt differently when I hadn't even 1 million because, after all, what do you need? It doesn't make any difference. You may have access to better facilities, but it doesn't change your life. It doesn't change your thought process. What makes me really happy is that I have been able to create a truly global steel company which is unique. This is a matter of pride and happiness to me. Whether you have money or not, happiness is the key.'

The 'better facilities' include a Gulfstream jet and a mansion in London's Kensington Palace Gardens, which he bought from Formula One billionaire Bernie Ecclestone for a reputed £70 million. It has twelve bedrooms, a jewel-encrusted swimming pool, a ballroom, and a garage for twenty cars.

Lakshmi was born into a steel-making family in India's desert state of Rajasthan. He studied accountancy while working for the firm and gained a degree. His first venture outside the country began with an unexpected trip to Indonesia. His father had bought a site there, with a view to setting up a steel plant, but later had second thoughts and asked his 25-year-old son to sell it. Lakshmi was on his way to a holiday in Japan but agreed to handle the negotiations. The sale never happened because he concluded that it would be a mistake to abandon the project. He called Dad, who said: 'Yes, okay, if you can solve the problems that's fine.'

His strategy since then has been to acquire companies at good prices, sometimes from national governments (as in the case of the Ukraine), to make them work better. Today Mittal Steel is a world leader in the market, and although it is quoted on the American and Dutch stock exchanges, the company is still 88 per cent controlled by the family and trusts.

Lakshmi is a much-admired role model for other Asian immigrants. They are usually said to be part of the 'ethnic minority', but many dislike the label because it is so widely associated with racism. As one Indian friend told me: 'White English people who live in former colonies could also be described as an ethnic minority, but they don't see it that way. I don't want to be called a British Asian – I am British, full stop.'

Not everyone feels as strongly about this as he does, but I can see his point because I am also an immigrant who chose to become a British citizen many years ago. Having a white skin made it easier to assimilate, but as a foreigner from a working-class background I encountered other forms of prejudice. I changed my name because I wanted to 'fit in' and disguised my working-class origins by learning to speak BBC English. Some of my friends said that I took the adoption of a British persona to extremes. There is a splendid but probably apocryphal story of the archetypal German immigrant who became 'more English than the English'.

73

After innumerable obstacles he finally receives his natural-
isation papers some years after the war, as I did, and bursts
into tears.

'Don't worry, old boy', everyone tells him. 'There's no
longer anything to worry about.'

'I know', blubbers the new citizen, 'but why did we have to
lose India?'

Today, of course, people from other countries in the
European Union can live and work in Britain without giving
up their nationality. People from outside the EU don't have
the same right, and many white Brits wants to see even tighter
curbs, but we *need* skilled immigrants to keep the economy
growing.

Opposition to immigration, however unattractive its
expression, is rooted in human nature. It springs from fears,
both rational and irrational. Individuals are unsettled by the
changes to the familiar contours of their community which
migrants bring. At its heart, the debate is not about economics
but about race.

What is often forgotten, or deliberately ignored, is that
many 'British Asians' were born here. They are the children,
and grandchildren, of migrants and are entitled to insist on
being treated as native Brits. Whites who complain about the
alleged loss of 'cultural identity' should spell out what they
mean by it and also consider to what extent that loss is due
to an entirely different factor – the pervasive influence of
American culture. The English language has become
increasingly Americanised, and millions of us watch Hollywood films and TV series rather than home-made products,
eat hamburgers rather than fish and chips, and worship
American entertainers. I don't mind, but it seems to me
hypocritical to talk about our cultural identity when so much
is not British at all.

There is a slogan you may have come across: 'money is

colour blind'. It certainly applies to billionaires like Mittal, but research has shown that non-whites still find it harder to get well-paid jobs in large corporations or to raise money for start-ups. It is one of the main reasons why many are self-employed and draw on families and friends for labour and capital.

The Department of Trade and Industry estimates that there are 250,000 'ethnic minority businesses' in Britain and that they contribute £15 billion a year to the economy. Many are small, and likely to stay small, but there are also many which have grown to a substantial size. Khalid Darr, Chairman of the Institute of Asian Professionals, says that 'entrepreneurship, coupled with a wonderful work ethic, fuelled by a desire to better oneself, is a potent force driving the British Asian community. Other sectors of the economy could do worse than study our methods and resolve.'

Various attempts are made each year to compile an 'Asian rich list'. It isn't easy, because so many companies are family affairs. There is also disagreement about who should be included. The *Daily Telegraph*, which publishes a version in partnership with *Eastern Eye*, leaves out people like Mittal because their business interests are largely overseas. (Another omission is Anurag Dikshit, a co-founder of the internet gambling firm PartyGaming. The *Sunday Times* list makes him the third richest man, with a fortune of £1.7 billion. He lives in Gibraltar, which many would argue is part of Britain.)

High on *everyone's* list are the four Ugandan-born Jatania brothers, who run a clutch of personal-care brands. Their company, Lornamead, was started in 1978 by George Jatania, the eldest, and has grown by acquiring what they call 'corporate orphans' – products that are being neglected – and adding value to them. In 2005, for example, they bought Yardley for a reported £60 million. The business is now run by Mike, the youngest. It has its headquarters in Dubai but they all have homes in London. The family has an estimated fortune of £650 million.

Next in line, according to the *Telegraph*, are the Patel brothers, Vijay and Bikhu, who own Waymade Healthcare. They arrived from Kenya in 1967 with just £75 in their pockets. Vijay enrolled at a London college and studied for exams in physics, chemistry and biology, washing dishes in a restaurant at night to earn money. He gained a degree at the College of Pharmacy in Leicester, and in 1975 opened a chemist shop in Leigh-on-Sea, Essex. By 1982 he owned six shops. He later focused on the distribution and development of medicines; Bikhu, who had trained as an architect, joined the company 'to give it some financial discipline'. Both are married with children and live near each other in Essex. They employ 700 people and are reckoned to be worth £440 million.

'When you start from zero', says Vijay, 'you have only one way to go and that's up. There is a hunger in your belly to succeed. My brother and I were determined to better ourselves and Britain was the land of opportunity.'

Third on the *Telegraph*'s list is Lord Swraj Paul. Born in Jalandhar, Punjab, he was educated at Punjab University and later gained a degree in mechanical engineering from the Massachusetts Institute of Technology in the US. He came to Britain in 1966 and established his first business, Natural Gas Tubes. Gradually he bought other units and in 1978 formed the Caparo Group, as a holding company for his investments in engineering and property development. He was made a life peer in 1996 and also has honorary degrees from several universities. Lord Paul has written a biography of Indira Ghandi, who awarded him the Padma Bhushan, India's equivalent to a British peerage. The management of his business empire is now in the hands of his three sons, one of whom is expanding its Contemporary Hotels operation. The family is said to be worth £450 million.

Another wealthy Asian is Surinder Arora. His parents gave him away at birth in India but reclaimed him when they emigrated to Britain. He went to a comprehensive school in Acton, West London, where he learnt English, and then got a job with British Airways as an office junior. Later he was a salesman at Abbey National, rising to become branch manager. In what spare time was left he pushed the family savings into property, eventually developing a row of houses near Heathrow into bed-and-breakfast accommodation. Today Surinder has the biggest family-run, independent hotel chain in Britain, including purpose-built hotels at Heathrow, Gatwick and Manchester. He also owns a chunk of Wentworth, the prestigious golf club in Surrey.

'It's all sheer hard work, I promise you', he told Andrew Davidson of the *Sunday Times* in an interview published in March 2006. 'Here you can work really hard and you can achieve something, which is so different to other parts of the world.' He certainly puts in long hours, but he could not have achieved so much, in so short a time, without strong backing from his main banks, Allied Irish and Royal Bank of Scotland. He also has a knack for finding other partners – he teamed up with Richard Caring, the clothing tycoon, for the Wentworth deal and the Manchester hotel is a joint venture with Cliff Richard, who was introduced to him by a mutual friend.

The Arora family is said to have assets of £100 million, but as in so many other cases there is a considerable amount of guesswork in the calculation. What is not in doubt is that Surinder is very rich. There is another quote from the Davidson interview which says a lot about him. What he learned from his 'good old mum', he said, 'is never get big-headed, be hard-working, never be shy, never be ashamed. And even if I am back to sweeping rooms tomorrow I never will be.'

Several other entrepreneurs have made serious money in the fashion industry. One of the best known is Shami Ahmed, the founder of the Joe Bloggs clothing label. Born in Pakistan, he was brought to England by his parents when he was a young child. His father set up a market stall in Burnley and Shami left school at sixteen to work for him. The business grew into a thriving high-street concern but Shami, not happy with retail, pushed his father into the wholesale trade. His mother and sisters ran the stores while they developed their plans. A millionaire at 24, Shami went on to launch Bloggs in 1985. 'It was a brand I just thought of by accident', he once told students at a business studies class. 'Everyone laughed and I thought that was a good enough reaction for me, because at least I got a reaction.'

He based his business in Manchester, which was on the upswing as the north's foremost centre for youth, fashion and street culture. Bloggs quickly became a household name, enabling him to become the first person to take a British firm into the UK top ten jeans brands. It now sells worldwide, with showrooms in London and across the Continent, in the Middle East, Russia, Malta and South Africa. In the 1990s, he also formed a partnership with Elizabeth Emanuel (made famous as the designer of Princess Diana's wedding dress in 1981) but it broke up and he took the label with him. Emanuel later brought a legal case to regain the right to her name, but the Trade Mark Registry ruled against her. He plans to license the brand to market perfumes and luxury goods. Shami and his family are reputed to be worth more than £100 million.

Manchester is also the base of Rajan and Sanjay Kumar, who run the Rajan Group, an international fashion distribution empire. Their father started the business in 1967 with an investment of £33 and is still Chairman. The brothers graduated from Salford University and then joined him. They are now the main shareholders and, in addition, manage a substantial property portfolio. The company supplies clothes to high-street chains, such as Zara, and has other offices in New York, Dusseldorf and Madrid. The family is said to have a fortune of £80 million.

Other successful Asians include Sir Gulam Noon, who has done more than anyone else to bring Indian curries within the reach of supermarket shoppers. He started his business in 1989 with three dishes – Chicken Korma, Chicken Tikka Masala and Beef Roganjosh. Now there are 140 and, he says, the Indian food industry in Britain is worth billions. Tony Blair nominated him for a peerage, but Noon withdrew his name after a fuss was made about his loans to the Labour Party.

Dr Kartar Lalvani, whose advertisements for his Vitabiotics vitamin pills are often seen on the side of London buses, is now Lord Bilimoria of Chelsea. His company imports its ingredients from India, where it has also set up plants for manufacturing health supplements for local distribution. He says that he can't quite understand why the British should today be a little slow to take advantage of the booming economy of India when they did so much to build its original infrastructure over 200 years ago. He has established breweries as well as vitamin plants there and his senior staff, who go out to supervise operations, are British.

The wealthiest female Asian entrepreneur in Britain is Rita Sharma, who runs the travel business Worldwide Journeys. Born in India and brought to Ilford aged just ten months by her parents, she later went to a local girls' grammar school and then on to Sussex University, where she dropped out after one term of law. In 1986, she started her agency in a windowless room above Oxford Street: all she had was two desks and some phones. Today the company specialises in selling tailor-made holidays to affluent customers and employs more than 100 people. Her husband Rahul is in charge of finances and they live in a lavish home in Regent's Park. They also have property in India and the South of France, and are reckoned to be worth £96 million.

There are, of course, stories of failure as well as success. Many ventures have flopped because they were launched too hastily, or because the owners expanded too rapidly and could not repay their debts when market conditions turned against them. It can happen to anyone; hard work alone is not enough. The desire to keep everything in the family can make one especially vulnerable. It often makes more sense to go public and share the risks with outside investors, as well as turning part of the assets into cash. But there is no doubt that Asian immigrants and their descendants have had an extraordinary impact on British business. Many could easily afford to leave; Britain would be a poorer country if they did go.

CHAPTER 6

THE ENTERTAINERS

Many fortunes have been made, and continue to be made, in the world of show business. We live in an age of mass entertainment, and performers who hit the jackpot, especially in America, can earn millions in a relatively short time. Some do so while still in their teens.

Fame and wealth can be a heady mix, which many young people find harder to handle than they care to admit. Elvis Presley became an international celebrity in the 1950s but came to a tragic end at the age of 42, destroyed by self-indulgence. Countless others have suffered the same fate, often because their careers went into a steep dive and they consoled themselves with drugs and alcohol.

In earlier days, entertainers usually had to serve a lengthy apprenticeship, which kept them in touch with everyday realities. The pay was generally low and they were considered to be socially inferior. The star performers did well but they were not in the same league as the showbiz moguls who employed them. Today, young people with a modicum of talent can achieve stardom (and earn big money) almost overnight.

Many vanish from the scene within a year or two because the public has got bored with them. Publicity is a two-edged sword. It can lead to instant success but it can also wreck a career; there is an ever-present risk that the media will switch from adulation to relentless criticism, based on the celebrity's often messy personal life. This is what happened to Michael Jackson, hugely popular until he was arrested and charged with molesting children. He was acquitted, but the media attention did immense damage.

Entertainment is a highly competitive business in which people will do just about anything to get to the top. For every musician, actor, actress, or TV personality who achieves even modest success, there are thousands who get nowhere.

In America, the biggest market, young men and women leave their small-town homes every week and head for Los Angeles, the country's fantasy capital. It has a glamorous image, but the reality is quite different. LA is a tough city, populated by people with inflated egos who, far from welcoming newcomers, seem hell-bent on making their life miserable. The place reeks of ambitious insecurity. Many give up. Others have a brief taste of fame and spend all their income; when the offers of work stop coming they end up broke. Even those who have had a good run often lose a sizeable part of their fortune because they get involved in costly legal battles with discarded partners.

On the flip side, performers with staying power have become household names and are seriously rich. Pop stars like Paul McCartney, Mick Jagger, Elton John, Phil Collins, Rod Stewart, Madonna and Eric Clapton have been going for decades, and are still making the kind of money others dream about.

For many artists, giving live performances is more lucrative than making recordings. The worldwide pop-concert business grossed $2.6 billion in 2005. With so many channels on TV, and a seemingly infinite number of choices on the internet, it would be easy to assume that theatres and concert halls are chronically empty. The opposite is true. Wherever you look, it seems, people want to see something – and someone – in person.

Opera singers like Luciano Pavarotti and Placido Domingo also got into the act of giving huge, profit-turning concerts some years ago. Their first joint performance, in a vast and ancient outdoor stage in Rome, was a great success. Snobbish critics were appalled, but the audience loved it. A staggering 10 million records of that event, and 1.5 million videos, were sold during the next two years. Other concerts followed and were also highly lucrative.

Merchandising has added a new dimension to showbiz. Hollywood doesn't just make movies; it also sells branded products. Toys, clothes, books and games based on characters and themes can bring in a lot of additional revenue. But producing films is expensive. Studios frequently spend more than $100 million on a single movie, without any guarantee that they will recoup their investments, let alone make a profit. Part of the reason, of course, is that stars with a good track record – people like Tom Cruise and Julia Roberts – demand such substantial pay. Their bargaining power has made them wealthy and many have accumulated assets that will give them a sizeable income in their later years.

However, some stars, including British actors such as Michael Caine, have always recognised that Hollywood is fickle, and have turned to other ventures. When I first met Michael in Los Angeles, back in the 1980s, he was already a partner in a trendy London restaurant, Langan's, and said that he was planning to invest in others. 'I grew up in the kitchen of big houses because my mother was a cook', he told me. 'I was a bit of the old *Upstairs, Downstairs* thing, y' know, like the television series. And I am a good cook. A very good cook, in fact, but having a posh restaurant in the West End, that was something else.' When he later decided to live in London again, he got involved in several new ventures. He said that restaurants were a branch of showbiz. 'You can go there and eat after a show, you can go there and eat before a show. Even better, you can go there instead of a show. The restaurant is the occasion.'

He is now Sir Michael Caine, one of a growing number of performers who have been honoured by the Queen. (The prime minister of the day actually decides who should become a knight or dame, but Her Majesty hands out the gongs.) Others include Sean Connery, Elton John, Mick Jagger, Tom Jones and Roger Moore. The official reason is usually that their services to showbiz merit recognition, but titles can also be acquired by contributing to charitable causes. The Establishment doesn't approve but most people are glad to see old class distinctions eroded.

The lavish lifestyles of many stars fascinate the public. The flamboyant Elton John, for example, has a number of luxurious homes dotted across the globe – a Windsor mansion, a London townhouse, a sprawling pile in the South of France, a palazzo in Venice, and a penthouse in Atlanta. He and his partner, David Furnish, have long hosted an annual ball in Windsor, and when they tied the knot in 2005 (after the ban on same-sex ceremonies had been lifted), he spent £1 million on a reception for 700 guests. But he also gives generously to charity.

Elton is 59, an age when many of us think about retirement, and could well afford to take it easy. He is said to be worth more than £200 million. But he is still much in demand, particularly in America, and clearly enjoys his fame and fortune.

THE BEATLE

The world's wealthiest pop star, Paul McCartney, also continues to work hard. Many of us remember his classic, 'When I'm 64', written when he was one of the Fab Four – a group of exuberant performers who called themselves The Beatles. It was a long time ago (they split up in 1970) but the songs he and the late John Lennon wrote remain hugely popular. Paul is now 64, but he doesn't have to worry about who will need or feed him. His fans flock to his concerts and he has a fortune estimated at £800 million.

His lifestyle is different from that of performers like Elton. He has always said that he prefers mucking about on his farms in Sussex and Scotland to hobnobbing with other celebrities. He likes to be seen in t-shirts and jeans rather than designer outfits. But when he goes on tour he has a large entourage, including bodyguards.

In 2005, the ageing star gave 37 concerts in America. In Boston, a 16,500-strong audience cheered as he serenaded them with old Beatles favourites and some of the songs he has produced since. As a curtain-raiser, they were presented with a 'home video' of his life and times. Here, in black-and-white footage, was the Liverpool he was born into in 1942 – a terraced and cobbled city haunted by the drone of air-raid sirens. There were images of Paul playing with the Quarrymen as a fresh-faced teenager. Then the audience was whisked through the sixties, when screaming girls invaded airports, and into the seventies when The Beatles were gone and he had his own group, Wings. He also answered the question which many people had asked him: why do you keep on doing it? His reply, he said, was: 'Come to one of our shows. You'll see why we keep doing it.'

What he meant is that he still loves to entertain and gets a buzz from the rapturous applause of an audience. Writing songs is a lonely business; Paul, like Elton and others, wants to be up there on the stage, even if it involves doing old stuff for the umpteenth time. His fans may no longer be screaming teenagers – some are now grandparents – but for them he remains an idol. Their memories are indelibly linked with the Beatles, and they will pay whatever it takes to see and hear the most eminent survivor.

The money is nice, but for Paul it is plainly of secondary importance. All he needs is Love. He found it with his first wife, Linda, and was devastated when she died after nearly 30 years of marriage. His second marriage, to Heather Mills, did not work out – the couple separated less than four years after their wedding.

GOLDEN OLDIES

Some of the other famous British stars have also shown remarkable staying power. Mick Jagger, Keith Richards, Rod Stewart and Tom Jones all remain at the top in their sixties. Jagger is reckoned to be worth £205 million and his fellow Rolling Stone, Keith Richards, is not far behind. ('Retire? I can't spell the word', the guitar legend said recently.) Gravel-voiced Rod Stewart tried his hand as a footballer and then as a grave-digger, before his musical career took off in 1969 when he was lead singer with The Faces. As a solo artist, he has had many worldwide hits and still earns big money from his performances. He has seven children by different wives and homes in Epping Forest, Palm Beach and Beverly Hills. Tom Jones, a Welsh miner's son, had his first hit with 'It's Not Unusual' in 1965, and continues to wow audiences in play-grounds like Las Vegas. He married his childhood sweetheart Linda 48 years ago and they have stayed together. Their substantial assets include a huge Los Angeles estate. The *Sunday Times* estimates that he is worth £185 million.

MR MUSICAL

Andrew Lloyd Webber, who has composed the score for so many successful shows, was brought up in an environment dominated by music. His father, Dr William Lloyd Webber, was a distinguished organist and principal of the London College of Music. His mother was a noted piano teacher and his brother Julian is a fine cellist. But, he says, the biggest influence was his Aunt Vi, who took him to matinée performances of every musical produced in London in the 1950s and who was on first-name terms with many of the stars. At the age of eight, Andrew began to devise his own shows, using a model theatre he had built himself, complete with a revolving stage made from an old gramophone turntable. This enthusiasm for the stage continued right through school and Oxford: he says that he considers himself lucky to have known, early on, what he wanted to do with his life.

While at Oxford he met Tim Rice, a fellow student who felt the same about the theatre and who had a gift for writing lyrics. They were soon working together. Their first hit was a pop oratorio, *Joseph and the Amazing Technicolour Dreamcoat.* The Biblical theme surfaced again in their later work *Jesus Christ Superstar.* Neither, however, made much money for them. Andrew has since told me that their biggest mistake was to leave the financial side to others. It made him realise that, if he wanted to do better in future, he had to set up his own production company – which he went on to do.

They had a hit with *Evita,* a near-opera based on the tempestuous life and times of Eva Peron. The idea was Tim's, but Andrew had the satisfaction of hearing people singing and whistling 'Don't Cry for Me Argentina' wherever he went in the world. That one song alone made him rich, but his enthusiasm for new projects was undiminished. He had the idea for *Cats* when he bought a copy of T.S. Eliot's poems at

Heathrow airport and read it on a flight to Los Angeles. It was an unlikely subject for a musical and he had trouble finding backers, but it turned out to be another big success on both sides of the Atlantic.

The partnership with Tim didn't last, but he went on to create more musicals with other collaborators. Some have not been as profitable – *The Beautiful Game, Whistle Down the Wind, By Jeeves* – but *Phantom of the Opera* has been a phenomenal money spinner.

Andrew used earnings from the show to buy a string of London theatres through his company, the Really Useful Group. But owning theatres is an expensive and worrisome business and he got involved in so many other ventures, including films, that there was little time for composing.

Lord Lloyd Webber (as he now is) has made a vast fortune but at 58 feels that he still has a long way to go. He holds a private music festival each year at his country house, Sydmonton, so that he can explore new ideas with friends. He also does a lot of travelling.

Some critics, particularly in Britain, have dismissed him as a poor man's Puccini or a 'one tune a show' merchant – perhaps due to snobbery and envy. It used to upset him, but he has come to accept that not everyone likes his work. What really matters is that millions of people around the world love it; no other composer has enjoyed such a huge following in his lifetime.

Mozart was a genius but he died penniless and was buried in a pauper's grave. That isn't going to happen to Lloyd Webber.

THE IMPRESARIO

Another Brit who has become super-rich in a field once dominated by Americans is Sir Cameron Mackintosh. He worked closely with Andrew on *Cats* and *Phantom of the Opera* but has also produced other hits, such as *Miss Saigon* and *Les Miserables*, and owns some of London's best-known theatres.

Cameron is good at spotting potential winners, which is harder than it may seem. He shared Andrew's enthusiasm for *Cats* at a time when many sceptics thought that it was bound to fail, and played a key role in proving them wrong. *Miss Saigon* was also regarded as a bad idea: who wanted to be reminded of America's humiliating defeat in Vietnam? And how about *Les Miserables*? An off-putting title and a subject that was reckoned to have little appeal for a mass audience. The main action takes place during the 1832 insurrection in France against an oppressive monarch, and follows the pursuit of a fugitive policeman. The musical is 'sung-through' (there is no dialogue) and the reformed criminal Jean Valjean, having unwittingly driven his persecutor to suicide, is transfigured in death and acclaimed by the souls of departed characters and *les miserables* on the barricades.

The show made its debut in Paris in 1980. Cameron heard a recording two years later and commissioned English lyrics. He persuaded Trevor Nunn and others at the Royal Shakespeare Company that it was worth doing, and the musical opened at the Barbican Theatre in October 1985. So far, it's been performed in 38 countries in 21 languages – a licensed school edition has seen more than 3,000 amateur productions. On the 20th anniversary, Cameron presented a special gala edition at one of his theatres and passed bottles of champagne among the audience.

He is a much better businessman than Andrew, with an admirable talent for staging spectacular shows and impressive marketing skills. One of his more recent ventures, a new version of *Mary Poppins*, was also a hit. The *Sunday Times* reckons he is worth £400 million.

Cameron lives in London and has other houses in Malta,

New York and Provence, but he regards his 13,000-acre Highlands estate as his second home.

THE FILM-MAKER

Ridley Scott, Britain's most successful film director, is a blunt-speaking Geordie from South Shields. As a teenager at the local grammar school, he considered acting. Instead, he became captivated by film-making. He enrolled at the West Hartlepool College of Art, wrote a script, and set to work with his young brother, Tony. They spent a summer holiday making a movie called *Boy on a Bicycle*. It was a modest effort; the big projects came much later.

When he left college, Ridley was awarded a travel scholarship and made a trip around America. He was particularly impressed by Hollywood and Las Vegas, where he saw stars like Elvis Presley, John Wayne and Dean Martin. On his return he began working for the BBC, designing sets and directing early episodes of the classic TV show, *Z Cars*. He also made commercials, which were so well received that he set up his own company at the age of 27. 'I didn't even think about making films for thirteen years', he says. 'Then I suddenly thought: "My God, I'm approaching 40, I'd better get a movie going."'

He created the superb *Alien* for 20th Century Fox in 1979, with an unknown Sigourney Weaver in the starring role, and went on to make *Blade Runner* and *Thelma & Louise*. He had a bad patch in the 1990s – some of his movies were box office disasters – but he was chosen by Steven Spielberg's company as the only man capable of directing *Gladiator* and its demanding star Russell Crowe. The epic was a huge commercial hit and won a best film Oscar. Other successes in this decade have included *Hannibal* and *Black Hawk Down*.

Tony is also in the movie business: he has directed films like *Top Gun* and *Enemy of the State*.

Interviewers often ask Ridley: 'What's the plan?' He says there is no plan. 'I pick up subjects that interest me and work hard at them. I make sure that the script is right before we start filming, pick people I can count on for the crew, actors who are not in love with themselves, and then just get on with it. I don't stop until I've got things right. Then I go on to what fascinates me next.'

He and his partner, a glamorous actress about half his age, have homes in London, Los Angeles and Provence. He is wealthy but dismisses the notion of slowing down. 'There are so many things to do', he says. 'Retire? You will have to shoot me first.'

THE TV PRESENTER

The world's richest TV presenter is Oprah Winfrey – her fortune is estimated at $1.4 billion.

Oprah was born in 1954, into the poorest possible circumstances. Her hometown was Kosciusko, Mississippi, in the era before civil rights when black Americans could easily be killed in the Deep South for trying to vote. Her teenage parents were unmarried. Her mother, Vernita Lee, was a housemaid and her father, Vernon Winfrey, was a soldier. She spent her first years with her grandmother, often wearing hessian overalls made from potato sacks. She was later sent to live with her mother in Milwaukee, Wisconsin. There, aged nine, she was sexually abused by her cousin and, later, by others. Not surprisingly, Oprah became a troubled teenager, once sent to juvenile detention home and pregnant at fourteen (the baby was prematurely still-born).

She moved in with her father in Nashville, Tennessee. He

decided that his errant daughter needed an education and she became an honours student. Her big break came when she won a beauty contest at seventeen. As Miss Fire Prevention, she visited a local radio station and, as a joke, read the news. The manager was impressed and offered her a job.

After leaving college, Oprah became the first black woman broadcaster in Nashville. She then took a job as a television reporter in Baltimore. But her bosses felt that she was more suited to working on their breakfast show. Viewers liked her and she had other offers: by 1984 she had taken over the AM Chicago TV show. Within a year she went national and *Oprah Winfrey Show* became the number one talk-show in the country.

She has been a superstar ever since. Her fans are over-whelmingly female; her critics are mostly men. I don't care for her touch-feely style myself, but I like her personality and admire what she has achieved. The show has spun off into a magazine, a TV channel, and a film production company, all of them furthering the Oprah brand. She can make or break careers. Her influence is such that recommendations from her book club automatically create best-sellers.

There is no doubt that her dreadful childhood has had a profound bearing on her attitude to life. She once told an interviewer: 'To have the kind of internal strength and courage it takes to say, "No, I will not let you treat me like this", is what success is all about.'

CHAPTER 7

THE CHAMPIONS

The world of sport has also changed dramatically. America is no longer the only country where stars can make big money. For many, the market is now global. Some are super-rich.

Take motor racing. Manufacturers like Renault, Mercedes, Ferrari, Honda, and Toyota spend vast sums on their Formula One teams, which compete in more than a dozen countries. They hire the best drivers and reward them handsomely.

Tennis is another international sport, with top players moving from one tournament to the next. And look at football. Earlier generations considered themselves fortunate if they were paid a decent wage. Today there is such keen competition for talent among European clubs that players have strong bargaining power and many employ agents to get the best deals. David Beckham, who now plays for Real Madrid, has his own company, Footwork Productions. Its sole function is to sell his services and he is the only shareholder.

Wages and prizes are bigger than ever before, but there are other sources of revenue. Many well-known organisations pay large sums for endorsements. David, for example, has made a fortune from a wide range of contracts. He has been the face of Brylcreem, and also endorsed Gillette, Pepsi, Adidas, Castrol and Police sunglasses. He and his wife Victoria are reckoned to be worth more than £80 million.

There is, of course, no guarantee that the good times will last. Sponsors want winners and they can be quite ruthless if a player fails to stay at the top. Age is a major factor – most performers have reached their sell-by date at 40.

It is still possible to make money later on. A famous name is an important asset. Jack Nicklaus created golf courses all over the world, and some tennis stars have launched their own businesses after leaving the professional circuit. Britain's David Lloyd built up a chain of thirteen clubs, floated his company on the stock market, and later sold his shares to Whitbread for £20 million. Others have invested in real estate. But there are also many former champions who have run into financial difficulties, often because they indulged in reckless spending during their peak years.

The great Joe Louis reigned as world heavyweight boxing champion for more than a decade but ended up as a penniless greeter in Caesar's Palace in Las Vegas. More recently, we have seen the decline of Mike Tyson. 'Iron Mike' was widely loathed, mainly because of his behaviour outside the ring, but in his prime he was a superb boxer who earned $50 million to $100 million a year. His friend Donald Trump frequently gave him financial advice but it was ignored. 'Mike', he says, 'was totally uninterested in money.' He recalls presenting him with a cheque for $10 million after a fight with Michael Spinks in his casino. Tyson said thanks and put it into his jacket pocket without glancing at it – it was no big deal. When Trump asked him a few days later why it hadn't been cashed, he shrugged and said he would look for it – but several weeks went by before it was found and deposited by one of his people.

In 1992, Tyson went to prison for rape. When he was

released three years later he fought another fifteen times, but he was no longer invincible and, after an ignominious defeat in 2005, finally called a halt to it all. 'I don't have the guts to be in this sport any more', he told reporters. 'I hate the smell of a gym. I hate the boxing game. The guy I used to be – I don't know that guy any more.'

Britain's Frank Bruno made millions from his title fights with Tyson (which he lost) but found it so hard to cope with retirement that he became mentally ill. His marriage fell apart and he was, for a time, held in a psychiatric hospital. 'All the trappings my career had brought me couldn't soften the blow of it ending', he later wrote in his autobiography.

Another British boxer, Chris Eubank, earned more than £10 million as a middleweight champion in the early 1990s, but was declared bankrupt in 2005 because he owed £1.3 million to the Inland Revenue and had other debts. 'Over the years', he said, 'I wish I had taken better advice. I appreciate this was my responsibility. I've made mistakes. Now I want to put this behind me and get on with my life.'

Boris Becker, who made a fortune in tennis, said much the same when he learned that a swift coupling in the broom cupboard of a trendy London restaurant, with a woman he had never met before, had resulted in the birth of a child. He not only had to settle a paternity suit but was also forced to give millions to his wife when she divorced him.

Some of the richest people in sport are not performers but owners and promoters. An outstanding example is Bernie Ecclestone, the man who created Formula One racing. An accident in 1951 ended his driving career, but he went into team management and eventually took over the whole of F1. He is a billionaire with a fabulous yacht, a private jet and homes in London and Switzerland.

In the US, many of the major league teams in baseball, basketball, and what Americans insist on calling football (even though it's more like rugby) are owned or controlled by wealthy individuals. In Britain, too, many clubs are in the hands of rich people who say they love sport but who often have other reasons for getting involved: status and, if their teams are successful, another chance to make some serious money. But let's take a closer look at some of the superstars with impressive track records.

THE DRIVER

Michael Schumacher ('Schumi' to his numerous fans) is widely regarded as the best driver in the history of Formula One. He is certainly the most famous.

The German has won the world championship seven times – more than anyone else. He hit a bad patch in 2005, mainly because Ferrari had technical problems, but he hasn't lost his enthusiasm for the sport and remains the team's leading driver. His contract is said to guarantee him $35 million a year. He also has a large income from endorsements and merchandising. His bright-red Ferrari driving suit is emblazoned with the logos of well-known companies.

According to some estimates, Schumacher has a fortune of more than $500 million. He doesn't get much chance to spend it because racing takes up most of his time; there are now nineteen Grand Prix events around the world. He did, however, donate $10 million to the tsunami aid effort. 'It's so unfathomable and horrible what happened to so many people', he said on his website. 'One cannot simply blind it out. We're suffering with them.'

The media has often criticised his aggressive driving style and tactics. Motor racing is a dangerous sport; one moment's misjudgement or misfortune could end his career or his life. Two former champions have died on the racetrack. But with so many rivals determined to get ahead (including his younger brother Ralf, who is paid $24 million a year by Panasonic Toyota) he knows that he has to take calculated risks.

Schumacher is a devoted family man and he will no doubt decide, at some point, that enough is enough. He has two children, Mick and Gina Maria. He says that he doesn't want Mick to go into racing. 'I'd prefer it if he played golf or tennis. It's tough imagining him following in my footsteps, if you think about what the media would ask of him and the pressure for him to get out from under my shadow.'

THE GOLFER

The richest golfer still playing in PGA tournaments is the remarkably gifted Tiger Woods. In 2005, he earned almost $12 million in prize money and another $75 million in endorsements and appearance fees. He has made more than half a billion dollars since he began his professional career in 1996 and many experts predict that he will be the first athlete to become a billionaire.

Golf lets players excel at a much older age than sports like motor racing, tennis and football. Woods is only 30 and intends to go on for many more years.

When he was born, in California, his parents named him Eldrick. His Dad later called him Tiger, after a Vietnamese soldier who had been a friend in Vietnam. The nickname stuck and turned out to be an asset: Tiger sounds more impressive than Eldrick. But he would have succeeded anyway because he is so talented.

His parents introduced their only child to golf by giving him a sawed-off putter to practice with. He picked the game up fast and won both the US Junior and Amateur titles while still in his teens. He went to Stanford University but dropped out to become a professional golfer. Jack Nicklaus said at the time: 'This kid is the most fundamentally sound player I have ever seen at almost any age.' Nike and another company, Titleist, took the same view and offered him endorsement contracts worth many millions. People were astonished by the riches thrown at such a young man – he was only twenty – but the sponsors were proved right when, the following year, he won the US Masters in his first attempt. He has since won many other championships and gained contracts from companies like American Express and Rolex.

His proud father has made the bizarre claim that he was 'personally selected by God himself to nurture this young man and bring him to the point where he can make his contribution to humanity. This is my treasure. Please accept it and use it wisely.' The media snickered but others believed him and established the 'First Church of Tiger Woods'. Their website is 'dedicated to examining the possibility that God is walking the earth as a 21st-century, multi-ethnic superstar golfer and whether that is any more or less likely than God coming in the form of a first-century Jewish carpenter.'

Tiger himself makes no such claim. He is a sensible, disciplined and highly competitive player who knows that it takes a lot of effort to stay at the top. He is married to a glamorous former Swedish model and has bought a 10-acre Florida waterfront estate on Jupiter Island for $38 million. It includes four houses and two boat docks, to accommodate his yacht. He also owns property in California, Wyoming and Sweden. Early in 2006, he opened a Tiger Woods Learning Centre in Anaheim. 'I can't believe that I have been out here for almost ten years', he said. 'Granted, my body feels it from all the wear and tear of competing and travelling. But the time has gone by quickly.'

THE GOLDEN COUPLE

When Andre Agassi married Steffi Graf in 2001, many people were surprised. The flamboyant American from Las Vegas and the cool blonde from Germany seemed to have little in common, apart from their love of tennis. But the marriage has worked and they now have two young children.

Andre had been married before – to the Hollywood actress Brooke Shields – but the relationship deteriorated when his career went into a steep decline. His world ranking dropped to a disastrous 141 after a bad run of matches and a number of injuries. The glory days seemed to be over and they split up. But a strict diet and training regime saw his return to form in 1999, and in June of that year he became only the fifth player in history to win all four Grand Slams. By the end of 1999, he was ranked number one in the world again.

Agassi was born into a sporting family in 1970. His father, Emmanuel, had won several boxing championships in his native Iran before emigrating to America. He enrolled Andre in the Nick Bollettieri Tennis Academy in Florida at thirteen, and the boy showed such promise that he turned pro when he was only sixteen. He quickly rose in the rankings and gained an early reputation as a headstrong maverick. His flashy outfits, designer stubble, pierced ears and long hair made him popular among young tennis fans, but did not go down well with the Establishment types who were running Wimbledon. They insisted that the young upstart should abide by the traditional 'all-white' dress code. He told them that he would rather not compete. When he eventually took part, four years later, Andre won the championship. By then he had also done lucrative deals, endorsing everything from tennis racquets to cameras and razors.

Agassi is greatly admired by ambitious teenagers around

the world and by the new generation of talented players. He has always had one attribute, which so many of his rivals have lacked – charisma. Even when he discarded the neon-coloured outfits, and his hair, he remained a great showman. His theatrical four-cornered bows after winning a match always earned him wild applause from spectators. Even the upper crust at Wimbledon recognised the need for stars who are loved by the crowd, regardless of their nationality. But the physical demands of modern-day tennis have made it increasingly difficult for a man in his mid-thirties to win major tournaments, and in the summer of 2006, after his final Wimbledon, he announced his retirement. Steffi called it a day long before, after an equally successful career in the sport, and has since kept a low profile.

The golden couple have made a lot of money. Steffi earned millions and Andre is reputed to have a personal fortune of $160 million. He intends to devote more time to his charitable foundation, which supports under-privileged children in Las Vegas, and to the building of the Andre Agassi College Preparatory Academy, a charter school for at-risk youth. He and Steffi have also gone into the real estate business. Their company, Agassi Graf Development, is building a luxury mountain hotel and private residences at Tamarack, a resort in Idaho. When he announced the venture, Andre said that they wanted to invest in something 'ahead of the curve'. Tamarack was everything they believed in. 'This is about family', he told reporters. 'About lifestyle. About four seasons.'

Their own children know how to play tennis, but whether they would wish to emulate their illustrious parents is another matter. They have seen how tough it is to reach the top, and the sacrifices that have to be made to stay there, and it would not be surprising if they decided to embark on a less arduous career.

THE SHOOTER

Some of America's richest athletes have made their millions in sports that don't have anything like the same following in other parts of the world.

I found it hard to understand the American public's enthusiasm for basketball until a friend in New York explained that he loved the speed of the game. He said that he couldn't see why the English were fond of cricket – it was so slow.

Golf and tennis are middle-class sports; basketball can be played by everyone. American children do it at home, with parents or friends, and improve their game at school or college. Professionals are heroes because they are capable of performing extraordinary feats of physical skill, accomplished with balletic and muscular grace. The enormous popularity of the sport enables the best to earn big salaries and to make the same kind of advertising deals as Tiger Woods and tennis players like Andre Agassi.

Until he retired in 1999, after thirteen years as a professional, Michael Jordan was the most famous of them all. Countless fans admired his athleticism, composure, court sense, fierce competitive spirit, and shooting touch from long distance. At his peak he was making $78 million a year and his personal fortune was estimated at half a billion dollars.

Jordan grew up in a working-class family in North Carolina. He later said that the greatest lesson his parents taught him was that race didn't matter. 'I never see you for the colour', he told reporters. 'I see you for the person you are. I'm recognised as being black, but I don't believe in race. I believe in friendship.'

When he announced his retirement, at the age of 37, he said: 'My responsibility has been to play the game of basketball and relieve some of the pressure of everyday life for people who work from nine to five, and I've tried to do that to the best of my abilities.' Many Americans still regard him as the greatest player in the history of the sport. The Chicago Bulls, his team for many years, put up a statue of him in mid-flight outside their stadium.

CHAPTER 8

THE DEAL-MAKERS

One can, of course, get rich without making things or providing a service to the public. An easier way is to deal in money. That, at least, is the impression conveyed by the media, which keeps telling us about the millions made by people who trade in everything from shares to financial instruments of baffling complexity. Many of the stories are quite true, but there are also many misconceptions.

The City, London's financial district, is still widely regarded as a British institution. This is certainly *not* true. The English gents who used to run the place retreated a long time ago; they chose to sell out to foreigners, who now play the dominant role. It is largely due to them that London has managed to retain its reputation as one of the world's leading financial centres.

If this is not as widely recognised as it should be, it is partly because the City still keeps up the trappings of a separate existence. Visiting heads of state are entertained in the Guildhall by a Lord Mayor in medieval regalia, flanked by pikemen in uniform dating back 700 years, and each November a new chap gets into an ornate coach and waves to the common folk. The British may work for Americans, Asians, Germans and other invaders, but many continue to dress up in robes and chains – symbolising offices that have no significance. The *real* mayor of London is a working-class bloke who makes no secret of his contempt for this tomfoolery.

The foreigners have introduced new ideas as well as funds, and they have had a profound effect on attitudes. Class has ceased to be important; the aristocrats have been replaced by international meritocrats who expect to be judged by what they do, not by their social standing. The City has also changed in other ways. Once known as the 'Square Mile', it now includes the Docklands, and the dingy offices of an earlier era have gone – the skyline today is a jumble of modern high-rise buildings, including the giant Gherkin.

Many of the big deals are made by investment bankers. They are deeply involved in take-over bids, mergers and other corporate activity. The fees they charge are often astronomical. They also trade on their own account. If all goes well, they reward themselves and their employees with generous bonuses. But things don't always run as smoothly as the media would have us believe. They may hit a bad patch because there is less interest in mergers and acquisitions, or because of a prolonged stock market downturn, or because they have made poor judgements. Even the self-proclaimed 'masters of the universe' are not infallible.

Some have got into trouble with the law (more about this later) and some have lost fortunes through reckless speculation. Betting on currencies with money is a high-risk game and trading in commodities has been compared to climbing aboard a big dipper which has no brakes or seat belts.

The new stars are hedge fund managers. Their job is to make rich people richer when the stock market goes up and to protect their investment when it goes down. Hedge funds are a diverse collection of investment funds, adopting all sorts of different strategies.

Small investors tend to be more familiar with unit trusts, which have been around for decades. (In America they are known as mutual funds.) Their most consistent attraction has always been that an investor, by putting up a modest sum, can participate in the advantages of a large, diversified and well-managed portfolio of stocks. It is a sensible approach and many people have benefited from it.

When unit trusts began to make a significant public impact in the early 1960s, there were some dubious ventures. One of the worst examples was Investors Overseas Services (IOS), run by a flamboyant character called Bernie Cornfeld. He had started as a salesman for an American mutual fund, but business in New York was tough and he decided to try his luck in Europe. Arriving in Paris with a few hundred dollars in his wallet, he soon saw the possibilities of a large expatriate market, especially American servicemen. He did so well that, three years later, he launched his own mutual funds and recruited an enthusiastic sales force. He devised an eye-catching slogan: 'Do you sincerely want to be rich?' Cornfeld also hit on what many of them thought was a brilliant idea: a 'Fund of Funds'. The aim, he explained, was to reduce the risks still further by investing in other mutual funds. The ordinary man would have professionals choosing the professionals who made the decisions. What could be safer?

His salesmen combed the whole world for people's savings and his managers put them into funds which IOS ran. But the products had one basic flaw. In the long run sales have to be matched by performance, and Bernie failed to deliver. The whole edifice eventually collapsed because the money was so badly managed.

IOS was, first and last, an organisation run by salesmen for salesmen. It was they who profited most from the vast flow of

money which the company handled. The 'financial coun-
sellors' did not have to be investment experts: Cornfeld told
them that after one week's training in salesmanship, they
would be able to go out and sell mutual funds to strangers
anywhere on earth. He gave them a text cast in the form of a
dialogue between salesman and prospect, which they had to
learn by heart.

'Mr Geldt', the pitch began, 'let's presume that you have
$1 million. You don't mind me presuming that you have a
million, do you?' (He didn't.)

It was then explained to Mr Geldt that if he really happened
to be a millionaire, he certainly wouldn't be keeping his
money in a bank. He would hire professional investment managers who would select numerous investment propositions
and spread the money out among them.

Computations were then produced, suggesting that a
mutual fund investor could expect to see $10,000 turned into
$54,000 within ten years. 'If that had happened to you, Mr
Geldt, would you have been pleased?', the salesman would
ask. ('Oh, yes.') And it wasn't even necessary to have $10,000
to put up at once. The prospect was told that just $100 a
month for ten years would result in a pay-out of $34,000.

Cornfeld, clearly, was a man who understood greed and
knew how to exploit it. One beneficial effect of his spectacular
rise and fall is that the industry has since been more tightly
controlled. There are many respectable funds, on both sides
of the Atlantic, which have performed well. But there will
always be an element of risk.

Hedge fund managers play in a different league. They are
not interested in small investors; their clients have serious
money. Many have billions under management and generate
impressive returns. A good 'hedgie' can earn as much as
$10 million a year in performance-related fees. But this is a
tough, male-dominated, macho world – in which the only

thing that counts is making the clients happy. Hedge funds involve much greater risks than unit trusts.

Most hedgies have their offices in the West End of London, not in the City, but this is a global business – in America, they operate in New York, Connecticut and other places. They also try to avoid the limelight. Few are willing to give on-the-record interviews, perhaps because their work can be controversial.

Another relatively new force is private equity. These are groups of wealthy international financiers who buy and sell entire companies. They have billions at their disposal and use them to make unsolicited bids. Once they have gained control, they shake up the management and cut costs. As private owners, they can pay themselves handsome dividends and escape the regular scrutiny of sales and profits which goes on in quoted companies. They can then sell all or part of the business, often via a stock market flotation, and make a substantial capital gain.

Some of the operations are run by the big investment banks. Goldman Sachs, for example, has an in-house private equity division known as the Principal Investment Area. Employees can participate: in 2005, they put $1.1 billion of their own money into an $8.5 billion buy-out fund managed by this division. But competition has made deals more expensive, and boards of potentially vulnerable public companies have become more adept at defending themselves against unwelcome approaches.

THE BLOOMBERG STORY

Much of what happens in the financial world is done in secret, but deal-makers and investors can access more financial and market data than ever before, using specialised computer terminals for swift and accurate information.

One of the first they should thank for this is a remarkable individual, Michael Bloomberg, now Mayor of New York. He has created a global, multi-product organisation with tens of thousands of clients, including the Bank of England and the Vatican. The public knows it mainly because the company also has its own television network.

Michael (he prefers to be called Mike) was born in Medford, a blue-collar community outside of Boston – his father was an accountant at a local dairy. He went to the city-run school and, while there, worked after class, on weekends, and during the summer holidays for a small electronics company in Cambridge. He later gained a degree from Johns Hopkins University and Harvard Business School. When he graduated from Harvard, he decided to embark on a career as an institutional salesman or equity trader on Wall Street. He got a job with Salomon Brothers and loved it; he was eventually made a general partner with responsibility for all equities.

For fifteen years, Mike worked twelve-hour days and six-day weeks. In 1981, however, the firm merged with a publicly held commodities trading group and he was fired. He collected $10 million as compensation and, at the age of 39, started his own business in a one-room office on New York's Madison Avenue. He recruited four former Salomon protégés and launched a company called Innovative Marketing Systems.

Many people thought that it was madness to take on the big players in financial news, Dow Jones and Reuters, but Mike was convinced that he could find niches that they didn't fill. He knew what traders wanted and set out to provide a value-added service that clients would pay for. The team devised a product, MarketMaster, which Mike took to Merrill Lynch, one of the top names on Wall Street. They liked it and ordered twenty of the terminals. Merrill Lynch eventually leased more than a thousand and also paid $30 million for a 30 per cent equity stake in the company, now called Bloomberg. Mike agreed not to sell products for five years to Merrill Lynch's major rivals, but the restrictive term was dropped when it still had three years to run.

By the late 1980s, Bloomberg had established offices in New York, London, Sydney and Tokyo, with more than 5,000 customers spread over 40 countries and an annual turnover of $100 million. It added other media services – a radio station, magazines, book publishing and Bloomberg Television, a global financial news programme with a unique multi-screen format.

Mike surprised many of his friends when he told them in 2000 that he was going into politics. He was elected Mayor of New York City later that year and delegated the task of running the business to able colleagues. He has since won a second term. 'I love governing', he says. He certainly doesn't need the salary that goes with the job – *Forbes* magazine estimates that the former trader has a personal fortune of more than $5 billion.

THE SAGE OF OMAHA

Not everyone wants to make it big on Wall Street or in the City. The world's most famous investor, Warren Buffett, prefers to operate from an office in Omaha, Nebraska. *His* net worth is reckoned to be $42 billion, making him the second richest man on the planet, after Bill Gates.

Buffett's father, Howard, was a local stockbroker and as a boy Warren often worked for him. At home, he began to chart the prices of stocks on his own and made his first investment at the age of eleven. He told friends that he was determined to become 'very, very rich'.

In the early 1940s, Howard won a seat in Congress and the family moved to Washington. Warren went to junior high school, and also did a paper route, but he was so unhappy in the nation's capital that he ran away. His rebellion didn't last long. He came back, graduated, and agreed to go to the nearby Wharton School of Finance and Commerce at the University of Pennsylvania. That didn't work out either. When Howard lost his seat, and returned to Omaha, Warren transferred to the University of Nebraska, his home turf. While there he read *The Intelligent Investor*, a book written by Benjamin Graham, a senior tutor at the Columbia Graduate Business School. Warren was so impressed that he enrolled at the school to study under him.

It was Graham who taught his ambitious young student the principles that, in the years that followed, made him very rich. Investors, Graham argued, should pay attention not to the tape but to the business beneath the stock certificates. By focussing on the earnings, assets, prospects and other essentials, one could arrive at a notion of a company's 'intrinsic value' that was independent of the market price. The trick was to buy when prices were far below intrinsic value and to trust the market's tendency to correct.

Warren set up his own investment partnership in Omaha at the age of 26. It was tiny – relatives and friends put in a total of $105,000 – and he ran it from his bedroom. He did well enough to attract the attention of other investors, including local doctors. By 1962, the number of partnerships had grown to 90, totalling $7.2 million of capital. Warren decided to merge them all into one, Buffett Partnership Ltd, and rented an office in Omaha's business district. During the next few years, he consistently beat the Dow by an impressive percentage. In 1969, however, he stunned everyone with the news that he was dissolving the partnerships because, he said, values had become increasingly scarce.

Warren had always taken a share of the profits, instead of a management fee, and had accumulated a personal fortune of £25 million. He was still keen on an investment he had made in 1962, a textile firm called Berkshire Hathaway, and now increased his stake to 29 per cent. He installed himself as Chairman and later bought more stock. Few people shared his interest in the company at the time; none foresaw that he would turn it into a giant empire.

Berkshire today owns 68 distinct businesses, as well as a massive portfolio of other investments. Its annual meetings have long resembled country fairs, in which the avuncular Chairman (dubbed 'the Sage of Omaha' by the financial press) plays host to barbecues, baseball and bridge games, and informal investment tutorials. Warren also writes chatty letters to shareholders each year, explaining what he has been doing and why, apologises for mistakes, and gives his views on market trends. The letters are laced with homespun wisdom, anecdotes, and jokes. Here is Warren on insurers who react to looming loss problems with optimism:

> They behave like the fellow in a switchblade fight who, after his opponent has taken a mighty swipe at his throat, exclaimed: 'You never touched me.' His adversary replies: 'Just wait until you try to shake your head.'

He also makes a point of paying fulsome tribute to his managers. Their positive attitude, he wrote in a recent letter, vividly contrasts with that of the young man who married a tycoon's only child, a decidedly homely and dull lass. Relieved, the father called in his new son-in-law after the wedding and began to discuss the future:

> 'Son, you're the boy I always wanted and never had. Here's a stock certificate for 50 per cent of the company. You're my equal partner from now on.'
> 'Thanks, dad.'
> 'Now, what would you like to run? How about sales?'

111

'I'm afraid I couldn't sell water to a man crawling in the Sahara.'

'Well, then, how about heading human relations?'

'I really don't care for people.'

'No problem, we have lots of other spots in the business. What would you like to do?'

'Actually, nothing appeals to me. Why don't you just buy me out?'

Wall Street's hot shots regard Warren as bit of an old buffer, but his track record and influence make the letters required reading. He often challenges fashionable concepts. For instance, he views derivatives as 'financial weapons of mass destruction, carrying dangers that, while now latent are potentially lethal'.

He says that he learned this the hard way, after one of Berkshire's companies ran up losses more than $400 million on its operation. 'The hard fact is', he told shareholders early in 2006, 'that I have cost you a lot of money by not moving immediately to close it down. It was my responsibility to make sure that it happened. Rather than address the situation head on, however, I wasted several years while we attempted to sell the operation. That was a doomed endeavour because no realistic solution could have extricated us from the maze of liabilities that was going to exist for decades. Our obligations were particularly worrisome because their potential to explode could not be measured. So I failed in my attempts to exit painlessly, and in the meantime more trades were put on the books. Excuse me for dithering. When a problem exists, whether in personal or business operations, the time to act is *now*.' He added: 'I hope that our experiences may prove instructive for managers, auditors, and regulators. In a sense, we are a canary in this business coal mine and should sing a song of warning before we expire.'

The 'canary' had ignored his cardinal rule: invest only in companies about which you feel absolutely comfortable, and knowledgeable. Choose a few stocks that are likely to produce above-average returns over the long haul, concentrate the bulk of your investments in that stock, and have the fortitude to hold steady during many short-term gyrations. This is what Graham had taught him, and the strategy had worked well in the past.

Warren ended his letter with some characteristically frank comments on his future. 'As owners', he wrote, 'you are naturally concerned about whether I will insist on continuing as CEO after I begin to fade and, if so, how the board will handle the problem. You will also want to know what happens if I should die tonight.' The second question, he said, was easy to answer: Berkshire had managers who were reasonably young and fully capable of being CEO. The other question that had to be addressed was 'whether the board would be prepared to make a change if that need should arise not from my death but rather from decay, particularly if this decay is accompanied by my delusional thinking that I am reaching new peaks of managerial brilliance'. It was extraordinarily difficult for most people to tell someone, particularly a friend, that he or she is no longer capable, but 'if I became a candidate for that message, our board will be doing me a favour by delivering it'.

Buffett, who is in his late seventies, still lives in the Omaha home he bought for $30,000. He has three children, but says that most of his fortune will go to philanthropies. 'They'll be wealthy, there's no question about that, but the idea of dynastic fortune turns me off', he says. 'The idea that you hand over huge positions in society simply because someone came from the right womb ... I just think it's almost un-American.' He has already decided to give 80 per cent, in annual instalments, to the foundation run by Bill and Melinda

Gates. 'They have', he says, 'committed themselves to a few extraordinarily important but under-funded issues, a policy that I believe offers the highest probability of achieving goals of great consequences.'

CHAPTER 9

THE PROPERTY GAME

Many property developers have made an enviable fortune but the stakes are high, and there are also many who have come to grief. The project may be in a location that turns out to have less appeal for potential customers than expected; contractors may cause problems; interest rates on borrowed funds may rise sharply; the market may go into a freefall; and backers may decide to pull the plug before the job is completed.

The first big-time developer I ever met, way back in the 1950s, was a colourful character named Jack Cotton. He had started his career in an estate agent's office at the age of eighteen and three years later set up in business on his own, with £50 borrowed from his mother. He rented a tiny two-room office in New Street, Birmingham, and ran the whole show single-handed. As time went on, he dealt increasingly for himself rather than for clients. He bought and sold land and houses, and eventually moved on to commercial development – where both the risks and the profits were greater. When I got to know him, as a young financial journalist, he had already created a formidable organisation, called City

Centre Properties. We talked in his 'office' – a suite in the Dorchester Hotel had become his weekday home and his headquarters (for weekends he had a splendid house on the Thames at Marlow). I was astonished to see lots of files spread out on his bed. 'My filing cabinet', he explained with a grin. He poured champagne – Cotton was a heavy drinker – and talked for more than an hour about property. He had a lot of theories but was also very much a man of action, and he had a powerful ally in Pearl Assurance, which held a quarter of the City Centre shares. One of his most ambitious projects was to create the biggest office block in the world. This became the Pan Am building in New York.

He later joined forces with another remarkable deal-maker, Charles Clore. They merged their property interests and, for a while, the partnership looked to be a great success. But the honeymoon was soon over. Cotton and Clore were both very independent individuals, firmly convinced of their own genius. Inevitably, they often had opposing views on how to handle a particular situation. Board meetings became increasingly bitter and they reached a point where they could hardly bear to speak to each other. Clore lobbied the powerful City institutions who had put up the money for the group's ventures and they agreed that Cotton wasn't running things too well. Three years after the merger, he was forced to resign as Chairman and chief executive. He sold his shares for millions but never got over the shock of being pushed out. He died of a heart attack, in the Bahamas, at the age of 61.

Another developer I got to know well was Nigel Broackes. He had worked as an insurance clerk but found the job boring. Was this his future – a lifetime in the City? His eyes fell on the huge office buildings going up all around. Now *there* was a business to be in. Exciting. Creative. Adventurous. And there was room in it for individuals – Jack Cotton had proved that.

But Nigel did not have the capital for big projects, and had little idea of how the game worked. He bought two old houses in Chelsea with money left to him by his grandfather and set out to convert them. 'Everything conceivable went wrong', he later told me. 'It took much longer than I had expected and I spent more than I had bargained for, so I didn't make a penny.' No one would have blamed him for going back to insurance. Instead, he decided that the best way to learn about the property business was to join a firm of estate agents. While there, he teamed up with a friend who was running an investment company in the City. Together they converted a building in Piccadilly and when that venture succeeded he left the agency to become a full-time entrepreneur.

Nigel went on to make audacious deals with the help of financial institutions. The business he and his friend had founded eventually became a public company, Trafalgar House, and he acquired other enterprises, including one of the oldest and best-known construction firms in the country, Trollope & Colls. I have mentioned him elsewhere in this book, but let me pass on his advice: do your homework, establish a reputation, be bold but realistic, make friends in the City (or on Wall Street and in European financial centres like Frankfurt), and choose partners who are not out to screw you.

Property speculation is a high-leveraged game. You borrow as much as you can and hope that by the time your loans have to be repaid, the assets will have appreciated so much in value that you can sell them for a handsome profit. It generally works when the market is strong but you can get into serious trouble if there is a downturn. This is what happened to many developers in the 1970s. The market collapsed without warning and they suddenly found that no one wanted to buy. They still had to pay interest, and meet their debts when they fell due, but the money wasn't coming in.

One of the most prominent victims was a Hungarian-born developer, William Stern, whose group was in the midst of building on 40 different sites in England. He ended up in the Guinness Book of Records as the biggest personal bankrupt in British history.

Stern had, until then, enjoyed a spectacular run. He managed to keep going for a while, but the downturn lasted for so long that his group couldn't meet its debts. When it failed to pay the quarterly interest on the loans, the banks brought in liquidators.

Stern's biggest mistake had been to give personal guarantees. It left him so exposed that bankruptcy became unavoidable. He had to live on support from members of his family for several years – he was finally discharged in 1985.

Many developers prefer to seek equity participation via the stock market or some other arrangement, because it makes them less dependent on short-term loans and they don't have to put their own assets on the line. But there are also still many companies that are privately owned.

One of the most successful young enterprises is London & Regional. It was founded in the late 1980s by a chartered surveyor, Richard Livingstone, and his brother Ian, a former optometrist. When the commercial property market hit another rough patch, soon afterwards, they were able to buy a valuable portfolio of distressed assets which they later sold to a listed group for a substantial profit. They re-invested the proceeds, buying empty buildings for development in Central London at a time when few were willing to take the same risks. The brothers have since expanded at a rapid pace – they are estimated to have developed about a million square feet every year. They own landmarks like the Hilton in Park Lane and the Empire cinema in Leicester Square, as well as office blocks and property in other parts of Europe, and are pressing on with a number of large-scale projects. Their net worth is said to be in excess of £250 million but they don't indulge in flashy displays of wealth.

Other players include the irrepressible Guy Hands, who made his name founding an investment group for Nomura, the Japanese bank, and in 2002 set up his own private equity business: Terra Firma. He retains close links with Nomura and has done some unusual deals, such as the acquisition of 230,000 cheap apartments in Germany. The residential market there, he says, is particularly attractive because it is the only one that has gone nowhere in the past decade. Sceptics maintain that there is a good reason for this: Germans tend to be less keen on home ownership than the British. Hands believes this will change. His approach, he says, is based on a careful analysis of social trends. 'Our objective', he told the *Sunday Times* in 2005, 'is to buy up to a million flats over the next five years. It will make us the biggest property company in the world.'

There are, of course, other contenders for that title – in America and in rapidly growing economies like China.

THE DONALD

The most famous developer of all is New York's Donald Trump. His name is emblazoned on skyscrapers and casinos, and he gets as much media attention as a Hollywood star.

'The Donald', as his Czech-born first wife always called him, *loves* being in the public eye. He has been featured on numerous magazine covers, written best-sellers with titles like *The Art of the Deal* and *Think Like a Billionaire*, and in 2004 became the host of his own television show – *The Apprentice*. (The BBC later launched a British version with Sir Alan Sugar.)

At one time he even considered running for President of the United States as a third-party candidate, but dropped the idea because 'I was enjoying my business too much to run for office'.

Brash, energetic, and ruthless, The Donald is an authentic New Money hero, a real-life soap character. The media has long been fascinated by his outsize ego, chutzpah, and flamboyant lifestyle. Here's how he kicked off the first season of the TV show:

> My name is Donald Trump and I'm the largest real estate developer in New York. I own buildings all over the place, model agencies, the Miss Universe Pageant, jetliners, golf courses, casinos, and private resorts like Mar-a-Lago, one of the most spectacular estates any-where in the world. But it wasn't always so easy. About thirteen years ago I was in serious trouble. I was billions of dollars in debt. But I fought back and won – big league. I used my brain. I used my negotiating skills. And I worked it all out. Now my company is bigger than it ever was and stronger than it ever was and I'm having more fun than I ever had. I've mastered the art of the deal and I've turned the name Trump into the highest-quality brand. And as the master I want to pass my knowledge on to someone else. I'm looking for 'The Apprentice'.

Trump's critics questioned some of the statements, especially his claim to be the largest real estate developer, but the public was smitten. By the end of the season, the show had 28 million viewers. The Fox TV network, owned by Rupert Murdoch, persuaded Sir Richard Branson to star in a rival series, *The Rebel Billionaire*, but its ratings did not draw anywhere close to those of *The Apprentice*.

The Donald is convinced that his many fans want to be just like him. 'I play to people's fantasies', he says. 'They may not always think big themselves, but they can still get very excited by those who do.' I'm sure he is right about that.

In one of his books, he acknowledged that he learned how to think like a billionaire by watching his father Fred Trump. 'He was the greatest man I'll ever know, and the biggest influence on my life.' Fred was already a millionaire when Donald was born in 1946. He had started building modest one-family homes in Queens, one of New York's boroughs, and used the profits to expand his business. His son would accompany him on tours of building sites, but he was such a rebellious teenager that Dad sent him to New York's Military Academy 'to straighten him out'. Donald says that it taught him to channel his aggression into achievement.

After his graduation, he spent two years at Fordham University and then transferred to the Wharton School of Finance and Commerce. He toyed with the idea of going into the movie industry but decided that real estate was a better business and, when he left Wharton, joined his father's company. One of his early chores was to go door-to-door in Brooklyn, collecting rents. He could have made a comfortable living but decided that he didn't want to be known simply as Fred's son, and he was not content with building homes in the outer boroughs. He wanted to try something grander, more exciting. To him, that meant making it big in Manhattan.

Fred did not share his lofty vision but agreed to give him a free rein. Donald was 25 when he moved into a one-bedroom apartment near Third Avenue and embarked on his quest. He soon discovered that 'making it big' wasn't going to be easy. His break came when New York went through a financial crisis in the 1970s; its debts rose to such an alarming level that many people feared it would go bust. Hardly anyone wanted to know about new real estate development. Trump shared the concern but saw an opportunity to acquire property at bargain prices.

One that he felt had great potential was a dilapidated hotel, the Commodore, next to Grand Central station. The owners asked him to put down a non-refundable $250,000 for an exclusive option, which he did with Fred's help. He eventually found a partner – Hyatt – and announced that he would totally rebuild the place. It would become one of the most glamorous hotels in Manhattan. The project took four years to complete, and there were many anxious moments, but when the Grand Hyatt opened in 1980 it was an instant hit. It established Donald as a man who could get things done, and it enabled him to go on to his next venture – a vast, glitzy building he named the Trump Tower. He is still immensely proud of it, and has both an office and a grand apartment there.

The Donald readily admits that he has a 'well-developed' ego, but regards it as a positive attribute. 'Show me someone with no ego and I'll show you a big loser', he says. *Time* magazine once called him a 'symbol of an acquisitive and mercenary age', which I expect he took as a compliment.

Early in 2006, he announced plans to build 'the greatest golf course anywhere in the world' after acquiring 800 acres of Scottish sand dunes. It would be known as Trump International Golf Links – naturally.

CHAPTER 10

THE CROOKS

Not all fortunes are made legally. One of the problems involved in trying to compile lists of the rich is that it's difficult, if not impossible, to include those who have made their millions through crime. The laws of libel are one reason. I can tell you about criminals who have been caught and found guilty, but I would get into an awful lot of trouble if I were to mention the names of suspected crooks. They all have expensive lawyers and would not hesitate to sue. The late Robert Maxwell frequently resorted to writs with the sole aim to silence journalists and others who suspected that he was up to no good. Britain has strict libel laws: they are designed to protect people against false accusations but, alas, also to protect shady characters like him.

I can, however, tell you about the methods still used by criminals today.

Countless Hollywood movies have dealt with bank and payroll heists, and with the activities of the Mafia. Producers and directors have cranked out dramatic portrayals of vicious little Caesars who gunned down anyone who got in the way of their relentless pursuit of a fortune. Mention big-time criminals to most people and they will automatically think of thugs like Al Capone and Mafia dons like the one played by Marlon Brando in *The Godfather*. There is no doubt that such characters still exist, but few would qualify for a place in a list of the richest villains. Things have changed a lot since the 1920s and 30s. The modern emperors of crime regard Al Capone as a foolish young man who made two bad mistakes: he loved publicity and he went to jail for, of all things, income tax evasion. The Godfather is considered to be an even more ludicrously old-fashioned figure.

I used to spend my holidays in Sicily and once went to interview a dozen alleged Mafia leaders who have been banished to the island of Filicudi. There was Rosario Terasi, who looked like Anthony Quinn; Calogera Sinatra (yes!), a sly, intelligent-looking man who struck me as capable of anything; Giacomo Coppola, a thickset, aggressive type with an immensely hairy chest; Antonio Bucellati, a short, powerfully built Sicilian who shouted every word and underlined his arguments with swift karate chops that made the table tremble; and a quiet, white-haired man who wouldn't give his name but told me in excellent English that he admired the late Sir Winston Churchill 'because he knew what he wanted and got it'. All had been in the construction business, a notoriously corrupt industry in which political influence was used, often with the help of bribes, to steer government funds into the pockets of Mafiosi.

Sinatra and the others, of course, insisted that they were innocent. The real bosses, they said, always managed to evade capture. This certainly appeared to be the case until they began to assassinate prominent judges sent by Rome to deal with them. Many were put behind bars for life, including the 'boss of bosses', Toto Rina.

In America, too, mob families are not as powerful as they used to be. They remain viable criminal networks but have been hurt by nearly three decades of prosecutions, mainly by federal authorities. There is much less violence than in the past.

The serious mob money is nowadays made, on both sides of the Atlantic, by drug dealing and smuggling. Gangs in countries like Colombia, Mexico, Russia, Turkey and Morocco play an active role in what has become a global business worth many billions a year.

Some crooks have turned to credit card fraud. One notorious case is that of Youssef Babbou, a Tunisian who assumed the identities of people whose names he took from rich lists. His principal target was American Express. He would ring a call centre in the US, pretend that their cards had been lost, and ask for duplicates to be sent to an address he supplied. He milked their bank accounts and travelled the world, staying in luxury hotels, hiring expensive cars, and buying Rolex watches and diamonds. Babbou was arrested in Paris, where he was found to have 25 false identities. The French extradited him to Britain and a court sentenced him to four years in jail; the judge ordered that he be deported on his release.

In Britain, the media still tends to focus on audacious heists. Everyone remembers the Great Train Robbery and there have since been many other capers, such as the Brink's-Mat bullion robbery. The gangs usually get caught and are sent to prison, but it has often proved hard to recover the loot. Only amateurs embark on an instant spending spree. Professionals find ways to hide it. They do their time and when they are released they pick up the stash and enjoy the good life.

Cash is the most anonymous kind of dirty money but it is bulky and easily lost, stolen or destroyed. The criminal cannot be sure that the stash will be intact after several years, especially if he has been foolish enough to share the secret with his wife or an accomplice who has been given a shorter sentence.

Small amounts can be used to buy jewellery and other valuables, which can later be sold. But large quantities attract attention and suspicion. A criminal can't just walk into a bank with a suitcase full of cash and put it on deposit. Banks are required to ask searching questions and to report dubious would-be customers to the authorities. Nor can he go to an estate agent and offer to pay cash for expensive property.

Professionals have, over the years, used other methods to obscure the real origin of their wealth. One of the most popular has been to use banks in one or more tax havens with strict secrecy laws. Switzerland, Panama and the Cayman Islands have long been among their favourite places. They would pay couriers to smuggle the cash out of the country in hand luggage or in a money belt strapped around the waist. The courier would go to a local bank and open an account. The bank would later be instructed to buy financial paper like stocks and bonds. The 'clean' money was then used to acquire legitimate business enterprises.

It is an enduring myth that the Swiss will gladly shield foreign criminals involved in narcotics, vice, fraud and other rackets. The charges are unjustified. All these things are major crimes in Switzerland and are taken seriously. The country is a charter member of Interpol and the banks are quite willing to cooperate with investigators if it can be shown that the depositor has been engaged in criminal activities.

Much has been made of the famous 'numbered account'. As the label indicates, a client is known by a number instead of a name. The arrangement is often said to have been invented to help criminals, but that has never been its purpose. Banking secrecy, and the numbered account, became part of Swiss law and practice only in 1934 to prevent Nazi agents from tracking down German money, largely Jewish, which had been smuggled out of the country and held in Swiss banks. The terrorist attacks on America, and similar events in Britain and elsewhere, have forced most tax havens to revise their secrecy laws. The ostensible aim is to deprive Al Qaeda and other terrorist groups of the means to conduct their murderous campaigns, but Western governments are also making a greater effort to go after other forms of organised crime, particularly drug trafficking.

There are still parts of the world where illicit gains can be hidden if the criminal masterminds pay large enough bribes. The international trade in narcotics like cocaine and heroin is so profitable that they can easily afford to corrupt politicians and officials, including the police. Many have their own Mafia-style 'soldiers' to kill people who stand in their way.

American authorities like the Drug Enforcement Administration are doing their best to cope with all this, but it is hard to operate in countries where they do not have jurisdiction and which will not readily agree to extradite their super-rich drug barons. Ronald Reagan, you will recall, had to invade Panama in order to capture Manuel Noriega, who as head of state had allowed them to function with impunity. Many have used their profits to buy land, real estate and companies in their own country, or to finance the election campaigns of politicians who can be relied on to give them an easy ride. Some laundered their millions so effectively that they have become significant shareholders in multi-national corporations.

Russian criminals have employed similar methods in recent years. At first, they were naive enough to believe myths about Swiss banks. They had been told that, in the Soviet era, many Communist leaders had accumulated millions in hard currency and used their political clout to smuggle cash to the West. The idea, apparently, was that they could leave the country if and when they were faced with events they could no longer control, and make a comfortable new life in one of the capitalist societies they claimed to despise. The gangs unleashed by the collapse of the Soviet Union thought that the Swiss would be just as eager to oblige them, and were shocked when some of their members were arrested in Geneva. They next arrived in sunny playgrounds like the Côte d'Azur and offered to buy property at exorbitant prices, providing the seller was willing to take cash. They had some success but this, too, turned out to be a risky business and more sophisticated methods are now used.

DIRTY COLLARS

Trading in narcotics is not, of course, the only way to make serious money. Fortunes have also been made out of white-collar crime, which takes in everything from embezzlement and fraud to stock-market manipulation and tax evasion. The white-collar criminal seldom resorts to violence, but depends chiefly on stealth, deceit and conspiracy. He is usually afflu-ent, and in many cases a pillar of the community. If caught, he tends to get lighter sentences than the common criminal, even though far bigger sums may be involved. In short, this is crime on a grand scale with relatively mild penalties and immense rewards. We condemn the drug baron, the train robber, the burglar and the mugger but often show a sneaking admiration for the clever individual who beats the system. We raise hell only if his manipulations score a direct hit on our pockets.

In the mid-1970s, a French-Canadian named Jean Doucet tried to prove that it's foolish to rob a bank when you can start your own and rob your depositors in comfort. He went to the Cayman Islands and set up two enterprises – Interbank and Sterling Bank. He pulled in a lot of cash, which he invested in his own projects. When depositors began to have doubts about those projects and asked for their money back,

Doucet left for Costa Rica in a Lear jet loaded with gold bullion. He later returned voluntarily to face prosecution and served just eight months in the island's tiny jail.

The principal ally of the financial swindler is greed. It makes some people extraordinarily gullible. They will believe almost anything, provided it's stated with enough conviction and holds out the prospect of easy profits. They forget, or choose to ignore, one of the older rules: if it seems too good to be true, it is.

Corporate fraud takes many forms but typically includes overstating profits, bid-rigging, establishing complex schemes that involve siphoning money into offshore accounts, money laundering and insider trading. Some of the greatest crimes in financial history were committed on Wall Street in the 1980s. The magnitude of the illegal gains was so large as to be incomprehensible to most laymen. The ownership of corporations changed hands, often forcibly, at an unprecedented rate. Many American household names vanished in takeovers that spawned criminal activity.

You may have seen the hit movie *Wall Street*, in which an unscrupulous trader named Gordon Gekko (brilliantly played by Michael Douglas) proclaims at a meeting of shareholders that 'greed is good'. The slogan was actually coined by a real-life operator, Ivan Boesky, but the Gekko character is also said to have been based on a fellow conspirator, Michael Milken. Both were eventually jailed, which is why I can write about them.

Until his misdeeds were exposed, Boesky was widely respected for his mastery of 'risk arbitrage' – betting on the outcome of business transactions. In a bid situation, the arbitrageur has to assess the chances of a deal going through. He may also buy stocks in a company which he only suspects could be the target of a takeover bid. If he has guessed right, the profits can be huge.

Many small investors try to play the game, but Boesky did it on a huge scale. At his peak, he controlled $3 billion worth of stock-buying power – enough to frighten any board of directors with a single phone call. He taught a course in the subject at universities and wrote a book about it. The financial press published flattering profiles of him. But the Securities and Exchange Commission (SEC) was not so easy to impress. It started an investigation into his activities and eventually charged him with insider trading – a crime because it involves trading in shares on the basis of information not available to investors generally. Boesky, it transpires, had made extensive use of his contacts in investment banking who were closely involved in planning bids and mergers, giving him a lucrative advantage.

The financial world was shocked when it was announced that Boesky had agreed to plead guilty and to pay a penance of $100 million. *Fortune* magazine called him the 'Crook of the Year'. Boesky thought that the penance would keep him out of jail, but when the case reached the courts he was sentenced to a term of three years. 'The signal must go out', the judge declared. 'The time has come when it is totally unacceptable for courts to act as if prison is unthinkable for white-collar defendants ... to preserve not only the actual integrity of the markets but the appearance of integrity in those markets. Criminal behaviour such as Mr Boesky's cannot go unchecked.'

Michael Milken's crimes were far more complex, imaginative and ambitious than mere insider trading. A graduate of the University of Berkeley in California and of the prestigious Wharton business school, he specialised in helping corporations to mount aggressive bids. As a student, he had done research on so-called 'junk bonds'. They were unsecured, high-interest securities which received low ratings from credit-rating agencies. He joined a Wall Street firm, Drexel Burnham Lambert, and worked hard to convince clients that these junk bonds were less risky than most investors thought. The firm began to issue large amounts of them. High-yield financing, as Milken preferred to call it, proved to be of immense value to bidders. Through his network, a raider organising a takeover could raise hundreds of millions or even billions of dollars in days. By 1986, Milken's bond empire boasted $125 billion in new issues. He was one of the most powerful men in American finance and one of the richest, with earnings in one year of $550 million. Part of this came from financing fees, which could be as much as $60 million on a single deal, but his close involvement in deals also gave him privileged information which he shared with Boesky: they agreed to split the profits.

Early in 1987, *Fortune* hailed Milken as 'the premier financier of his generation'. Others called him a 'genius'. What they did not know was that – as with Boesky – the SEC had decided to launch an investigation. It took a long time and much digging, but in April 1989 it had accumulated enough damaging evidence to bring charges. Milken pleaded not guilty to a 98-count indictment and hired a team of trial lawyers. They advised him to seek a plea bargain. The prosecution took a tough line and he finally admitted to six felonies and agreed to pay $600 million.

In November 1990, he sat in court, dazed, as the judge delivered her verdict. She told him: 'When a man of your power in the financial world, at the head of the most important investment banking houses in this country, repeatedly conspires to violate, and violates, securities and tax laws in order to achieve more power and wealth for himself and his wealthy clients, and commits financial crimes that are particularly hard to detect, a significant prison term is required in order to deter others.' She went on: 'This kind of misuse of your leadership position and enlisting employees who you supervised to assist you in violating the laws are serious crimes warranting serious punishment and the discomfort and opprobrium of being removed from society.'

There were gasps in the courtroom when the judge sentenced him to ten years in a federal prison. It was unusually severe for a white-collar crook. The story did not end there. Faced with the threat of further litigation, Milken paid an additional $500 million on top of the $600 million criminal settlement. According to some sources, it still left him and his family with a large fortune.

Like most people, I find it hard to understand why people like Boesky and Milken should have engaged in criminal activities when they had already made millions from legitimate deals. The short answer, I suppose, is that they were greedy and believed that they were above the law.

One would like to think that their punishment deterred others, but there have since been many more cases of dishonest behaviour. Some chief executives have used their company as piggy banks, or manipulated the balance sheets to make it look like the business was doing better than it really was.

Not long ago, the founder of WorldCom, Bernard Ebbers, was convicted of fraud and given a 25-year jail sentence. Another much-publicised scandal centred on two former heads of the energy giant Enron, Ken Lay and Jeffrey Skilling. Early in 2006, a jury in Houston found them guilty of the biggest corporate fraud in American history.

Lay, the son of a Baptist minister, grew up poor in Missouri. He went to university and gained a masters degree in economics. A series of jobs led him to Enron. He eventually became its chief executive and turned it into the seventh-largest corporation in the US. He flaunted his close ties to the family of President Bush and was inducted into the Texas Hall of Fame. At the peak of his career, Lay was one of the highest-paid bosses in the country.

It all began to go wrong when one of his employees, Sherron Watkins, wrote him a letter in which she warned that there were serious accounting problems. Lay refused to take her seriously, so she went to the authorities, who decided to launch an investigation. The media soon got on to the story. Enron had just reported a $638 million loss and was forced to admit to a $1.2 billion black hole in its balance sheet. A few weeks later, with shares that had once traded at $90 down to less than $1, Enron declared itself bankrupt. The company's collapse cost investors billions of dollars and sent shock waves through Wall Street and Congress. More than 21,000 people lost their jobs. The government stepped up its investigation but it took several years and sixteen weeks of testimony at trial to bring Lay and his co-defendant to justice.

Born in Pittsburgh, Jeffrey Skilling had a masters degree from Harvard and worked as a consultant for McKinsey before catching the eye of Lay. He later became his closest associate. Skilling told a congressional committee that he thought Enron was in good shape at the time it went under, but the prosecution convinced the jury that both men must have known their company was a house of cards (they had sold shares while encouraging others to buy) and that they were guilty of crooked accounting.

After the verdict was announced, the director of the Justice Department's Enron Task Force said outside the courthouse: 'The jury has spoken and they have sent an unmistakable message to boardrooms across the country that you can't lie to shareholders, you can't put yourself in front of your employees' interests, and no matter how rich and powerful you are, you have to play by the rules.'

Ken Lay died, apparently from a heart attack, before he

could be sentenced. He was 64. Legal experts said that his death was likely to block government attempts to seize his remaining assets but that his family could still face civil lawsuits. Former president George Bush and his wife Barbara attended the funeral.

In Britain, many of us still remember the shenanigans of Robert Maxwell, and of Nick Leeson, the young rogue trader who brought down Barings, one of the oldest firms in the City. There have been many other scandals – perhaps not in the same league as the crimes of Boesky and Milken, but that still hurt many people. In October 2005, two former directors of the software company AIT were found guilty of 'recklessly' misleading the market by making an inaccurate Stock Exchange announcement. The judge who sentenced them to prison said: 'Neither of you cared whether the information was true or false and were heedless of the consequences in the madcap hope that all would be all right on the night. It wasn't. Conduct such as this cannot be treated lightly by the courts, particularly in view of the message that needs to be sent out.'

In another case, a wealthy entrepreneur and former Chairman of Darlington Football Club, George Reynolds, was given a three-year sentence for cheating the Inland Revenue out of £650,000. Reynolds was reputed to be worth £260 million, so he had no need to dodge taxes.

The regulatory authorities on both sides of the Atlantic have stepped up their efforts to catch white-collar criminals and judges have clearly become less tolerant. Drug dealers and bank robbers can still expect to get longer sentences, but the message is getting across to the rich players of financial games: go bad and you are liable to find yourself sharing a cell with them.

Chapter 11

No Place Like Home

One of the greatest pleasures of the rich has always been the possession of impressive homes. There is something quite basic about the urge to live in a grandiose residence; it is a personal advertisement, a status symbol which tells the world that the owner is an important member of his tribe. The Roman nobles had the largest villas; medieval barons had massive castles; American Indian chiefs had the biggest tents. Comfort often had little to do with it – many were distinctly uncomfortable. The principal aim was to show that the occupant was someone special.

In Europe, monarchs set the pace and the aristocracy followed. Few barons dared to build an edifice that was bigger than the king's; there was always a risk that he would find some reason to confiscate it, as Henry VIII did when he saw Cardinal Wolsey's Hampton Court. But it was unthinkable that a duke or marquis should live in a modest house or, God forbid, in an apartment. If he lacked the means to build a home commensurate with his status, the government sometimes helped. John Churchill, the first Duke of Marlborough and one of England's greatest military heroes, was given the magnificent Blenheim Palace after his victory over the French in 1704. Glory wasn't enough; a grateful nation felt compelled to build him a home with 187 rooms.

When commoners started to make fortunes during the Industrial Revolution, they too wanted to show that they stood above the herd. The industrialist or financier was not content with piling up the cash; he wanted the world to see that he had arrived. In Britain, many tried to outdo the aristocrats. In America, which had no traditional ruling class, the new millionaires copied the stately homes of the European nobility. Many were immigrants from humble backgrounds who, in their youth, had looked longingly at the imposing mansions of the rich and titled. They could not buy a title, but they could certainly acquire some of the other trappings of the privileged class, so they not only built grand residences but also ransacked the art treasures of the countries they had left behind. Medieval castles were stripped of their carvings and tapestries, ornate staircases and ceilings were ripped out of stately homes which their European owners could no longer afford to maintain, and shiploads of Tudor chests and bedsteads, elaborate French furniture, suits of armour, statues, chandeliers, porcelain and paintings by Old Masters made their way across the Atlantic.

New York's Fifth Avenue became the premier showcase in the latter part of the 19th century. So many mansions and chateaux of French, Gothic and Italian style lined both sides of the two-mile stretch of boulevard that the newspapers dubbed it 'Millionaires' Row'. One of the biggest belonged to the Vanderbilts, whose fortune had been founded by 'Commodore' Vanderbilt, a ruthless robber baron who made his millions in the shipping business despite his lack of any formal education. Built in neo-Grecian style, it had a huge ballroom, a library, dining halls, salons, a gymnasium and a picture gallery, which occupied the entire rear of the house

1. The lure of wealth. Michael Jackson leaving court during one of several attempted multi-million-dollar lawsuits against him.

2. The Prince of Wales and his wife, the Duchess of Cornwall. Although already very rich, when Prince Charles becomes King, he is also in line to acquire most of his mum's assets.

3. London-based Indian billionaire industrialist Lakshmi Mittal, who is thought to have acquired an estimated wealth of £15 billion through the manufacture of steel.

4. A lady in waiting. Heiress to the Hilton Hotel and real estate fortune, Paris Hilton, with dog.

5. Hugh Hefner, the founder and editor-in-chief of *Playboy* magazine, is never far from the trappings of wealth.

6. Current owner of Express Newspapers Richard Desmond, who made much of his fortune by publishing a large number of pornographic titles.

7. Retail entrepreneur Sir Philip Green, who paid himself a cool £1.17 billion in 2005.

8. American golfer and highest-earning sportsman in the world, Tiger Woods. The millions he makes each year from prize money are dwarfed by the income from his collection of endorsement contracts.

9. Co-founder and current CEO of Apple Computer, Steve Jobs. Apple drove him away, but years later he made a dramatic comeback.

10. Gerald Grosvenor, 6th Duke of Westminster (left), who has an estimated fortune of more than £5 billion, in action for the Territorial Army.

11. Russian oil billionaire and Chelsea FC owner Roman Abramovich has enabled the Premiership club to buy players virtually at will in recent years, irrespective of the price.

12. Donald Trump, American real estate player and executive producer and host of reality television show, *The Apprentice*.

13. Many pets of the rich are afforded similar trappings of wealth to their owners.

14. Michael Bloomberg – founder of Bloomberg LP, the current Mayor of New York City and one of America's wealthiest men.

15. American record producer, actor, and general all-round entertainment mogul Sean 'Diddy' Combs, who presides over a media empire that includes his own record company, film production company, clothing line and chain of restaurants.

16. Karl Lagerfeld and Valentino Garavani, who have become rich by clothing the rich.

17. Robbie Williams, Victoria and David Beckham out enjoying their respective fortunes.

18. Veteran English musician Sir Elton John (seen here with civil partner David Furnish) is not known to be shy about dipping into his vast fortune.

and was filled with hundreds of paintings and sculptures. The drawing salon had ceilings painted by Gallaud of Paris. The massive frames of its doors were encrusted with gold and the walls were hung with pale red velvet, embroidered with foliage, flowers, and butterflies encircled with cut crystal and precious stones. Vases, upheld by female figures in solid silver, stood on pedestals on onyx with bronze trimmings.

Just about everything, including the beds, had been brought in from overseas. The result was a bizarre hash of styles – French tapestries, Florentine doors, African marble, English china, Dutch Old Masters, Japanese knick-knacks. The Commodore was delighted when *Harper's Weekly* called his palace the 'Taj Mahal of New York'; other commentators were less flattering.

The splendour did not last. The Vanderbilt residence was closed forever in 1945 and the other mansions of New York's 'gilded age' have also disappeared. But there are still many reminders of that period throughout America. Most are now museums. In Newport, Rhode Island, you can visit the 'summer cottages' built by the rich in the 1880s and 90s. They were actually more like palaces where they could entertain on a lavish scale. (A friend who still lives in the resort showed me around and then took me to the Newport Reading Room, one of the oldest clubs in the country. It was a modest little house where, he said, the robber barons would escape to when they got tired of all the social climbing; their wives were excluded from membership.)

One of the most famous pleasure domes is San Simeon, in California. It was built by William Randolph Hearst, the newspaper mogul on whom Orson Welles is said to have based the main character in his classic film *Citizen Kane*. Hearst decided that he wanted a mountaintop castle, overlooking the ocean, where he could entertain his many friends and acquaintances, including Hollywood stars like Charlie Chaplin and Douglas

Fairbanks. Like other millionaires before him, he filled his home with antiques and art objects he had acquired in Europe. He even built a large zoo on the property for the amusement of his guests. When Hearst died in 1951, his five sons and their families continued to use the castle for vacations but it was so big that they couldn't afford to maintain it. Unable to find any buyers, they donated San Simeon to the state of California, which turned it into a profitable tourist attraction.

The rich still like to have luxurious homes, but they tend to build on a smaller scale than their plutocratic forebears. Privacy is widely considered to be more important than the ostentatious display of wealth. In New York, today, many would rather have a sumptuous apartment at an exclusive address than a grand mansion. They want to impress each other, but they are no longer so eager to impress the public. Rupert Murdoch is said to have paid $44 million for a penthouse on Fifth Avenue that once belonged to Laurance Rockefeller. Others are owned by the heavy hitters of the world of finance, including British bankers. Showbiz celebrities have also bought upmarket flats for millions, but they are not always welcome. The city's notorious co-op boards (residential committees who have to give their approval) have rejected many stars because they feared the publicity and noisy parties they would bring.

Many rich Americans, and some Europeans, have a summer home in the Hamptons on Long Island. Only 80 miles from Manhattan, it not only has some of the country's best beaches and the blue Atlantic Ocean but also bays, inlets, and a collection of pretty villages, first settled in the 17th century by the Dutch and the English. 'New York without poor people', the Hamptons have been called, and it has never been more apt than it is now. The going rate for a really choice property is $25 million. The super-rich, who have domestic staff, rarely leave their compounds at weekends and can, therefore, enjoy the true delights of the place – no crowds, no queues, no proles.

Many also have a third home in London or Paris. They may use it only for the social 'season' but it's better than staying in a hotel and it makes them bona fide members of the international elite. London has become more popular than Paris because we speak the same language, more or less, and are perceived to be more friendly than the French. Some Americans, however, prefer to own property in Provence or Italy. They no longer ransack the mansions of the aristocracy – they *buy* them. Like many Brits, they are entranced by the sight of a crumbling chateau or a majestic Italian villa, which they are determined to 'do up'.

A relatively new status symbol, on both sides of the Atlantic, is ownership of a vineyard or olive farm. In America, this generally means buying a winery in California's Napa Valley. In Europe, Provence and Tuscany are the most fashionable areas.

One wine-maker in the Tuscan hills is a noted American porn celebrity, Savanna Samson. She is the star of more than 25 sexually explicit films but says there was something about them that left her unfulfilled. On a vacation in Italy, she told the *New York Times*, she was struck by something akin to an existential crisis. 'How can I leave a mark on the world?' she asked herself. 'And I thought: "wine".'

Other celebrities who have their own label include Madonna, the Rolling Stones, Sting, Mick Hucknall and Sir Cliff Richard. Sir Cliff, who has a vineyard in Portugal, told the *Daily Telegraph*: 'I've got better reviews for my wine than I have ever done for any of my concerts and albums. Clearly I should have gone into wine in the first place and not bothered at all with rock and roll.' Many of us would agree.

ISLAND HIDEAWAYS

Another ego trip is the ownership of a private island. The main attraction, apart from the prestige it conveys, is that the rich can be sovereigns of their own little kingdom. They don't have to put up with awkward neighbours and nosy tourists. Greek shipping billionaires are often said to have started the trend, but many wealthy American families have also had an island retreat for generations and today's owners include Brits like Sir Richard Branson and the Barclay twins.

There are more islands for sale than ever before, particularly in Asia and in countries like Canada, Norway, Finland and Croatia. You can even buy one that is man-made: a collection of about 300 has been created off the coast of Dubai in the United Arab Emirates. (Prices started around $7 million.) But turning an underdeveloped 'paradise' into a comfortable home requires a huge amount of work, patience and additional expenditure. Many islands have no water or electricity, building materials and workers have to be brought in by ship, and contractors are often unreliable. Other problems arise when the job is done – there are no medical facilities or shops. The privacy is nice but can get boring if one stays for any length of time. And you can't just leave and hope that everything will be OK while you are away. There may be storms, thieves or squatters. So you need to hire a permanent staff that will take care of your kingdom.

It often makes more sense to get some friends to share your escapist fantasy. This is what Lord Glenconner did when he bought the Caribbean island of Mustique. It became a refuge for a small circle of the rich and famous. The late Princess Margaret had a home there and Mick Jagger built himself a Japanese-style beach house. Other exclusive enclaves include Lyford Cay in the Bahamas. You have to be affluent to buy a house there, but money alone won't get you accepted: like

Manhattan's co-op boards, they have ways of keeping out people who are judged to be 'undesirable'.

The wealthiest small island in the world is Palm Beach, in Florida. This is where many of the seriously rich go when it gets chilly in the Hamptons and Europe. Less than four square miles in land area, Palm Beach has the largest number of centimillionaires (people with more than $100 million, also known as a 'unit') and the most impressive collection of ritzy homes. An oceanfront estate can cost as much as $70 million. Anyone can buy a grand mansion but it doesn't guarantee admission to the social A-list. Clubs in Florida, like Everglades and Bath & Tennis, are just as elitist as Lyford Cay.

The Palm Beach resort was 'invented' at the end of the 19th century by the oil baron and railway magnate Henry Morrison Flagler. One of his hotels, the Breakers, is still among the best in the sunshine state. It resembles an ornate Italian Renaissance palace and is, of course, expensive. He also built himself a stylish mansion, which is now a museum. By the 1920s, everything about Palm Beach was superlative. The rich sought to outdo each other by commissioning well-known architects to design opulent homes. One of the most impressive was constructed by Marjorie Merriweather Post, a breakfast-food heiress who married a wealthy financier. A Moorish palace of 50 rooms, Mar-a-Lago was surrounded by seventeen acres of lush tropical landscape.

Like the Vanderbilts, she entertained in royal style, sometimes importing the full production of a Broadway show for the evening. When she died in 1973, she willed the estate to the National Park Service to be used by the President and visiting heads of state, but this was ruled out for security reasons. (John F. Kennedy was, however, a frequent visitor to the island – the Kennedys had their own family compound.) Mar-a-Lago was eventually bought by Donald Trump, who turned it into a private club. Old Money people expressed dismay, especially when the flamboyant property developer told an interviewer: 'I'm the king of Palm Beach.' He says they are snobs who envy his success.

Today many of the homes are owned by the nouveau riche, including celebrities like Rod Stewart. They do much of their shopping in the stores, art galleries and boutiques on Worth Avenue, one of the most elegant (and pricey) showcases on the planet.

There are, of course, other places where the rich like to huddle together. Not everyone wants to be on an island. Many have a chalet or apartment in a classy ski resort like Aspen, Gstaad, or St Moritz. European summer playgrounds include old favourites like the Côte d'Azur. (But note that St-Tropez is over-rated: only the flashy crowd thinks it's smart.) A common factor, as we have seen, is the need to avoid tourists, especially in August. There are just too many of them, running around half-naked with their noisy children, invading beaches and restaurants which the rich regard as their own preserve, parking anywhere they like, and taking pictures of villas that are not protected by high hedges and long driveways. It was never like this in the 'old days'.

YOU MUST SEE MY PICASSO

Grand homes still require grand decor, but the approach to interiors has changed. People who have inherited their estates tend to hang on to suits of armour, mighty fireplaces and statues of Roman emperors, but most of the rich in countries such as the United States and Britain prefer a modern setting to the cluttering, swaggering pomp of the past. There is greater concern with quality than quantity, and much more emphasis on practical amenities. Americans and

Brits who visit Versailles for the first time invariably express amazement that a king who could build such a magnificent edifice managed to do without a single bathroom or even a toilet he could flush. For today's wealthy families, four or five bathrooms are a must and one should also have a jacuzzi, sauna and swimming pool.

The newly rich do not, as a rule, devote much time to furnishing their homes. They claim to be too busy, but the truth is that many don't know how to go about it. They are more familiar with balance sheets than with wallpaper. They want a home that reflects their status and which is comfortable, but are quite content to leave the job to a professional designer. Gilded mirrors and big sofas generally meet with instant approval. Antiques and oriental carpets are something else; a tycoon who is hooked on new products may find it hard to understand why he should live among old things. He gets even more confused when he is asked for his views on paintings. He has never bothered to study art but has always claimed that he knows what he likes; usually large paintings that 'tell a story' – battle scenes, pastoral glimpses and animals of all sorts. When confronted with a work by someone like Picasso he will either reject it out of hand or confess that 'I don't see what the man is getting at'. Designers can generally win the argument by pointing out that Picasso paintings are an excellent investment and that visitors will be impressed. (Picasso himself was well aware of this kind of attitude. He despised it, but was also shrewd enough to make the most of it. An American once spotted him at his favourite restaurant on the Côte d'Azur, where he was having lunch with friends, and asked him to 'draw something'. Picasso smiled, and with a few swift strokes covered part of the paper which served as a tablecloth. The American couldn't decide what, if anything, the drawing was supposed to mean, but was happy with the big signature and paid him enough to finance his meals for several months. No wonder he became the richest artist in history.)

Newspapers and magazines nowadays give a great deal of coverage to the investment aspects of works of art. Auctions are widely reported and there are tales galore about the stupendous increase in prices of everything from Victorian landscapes to abstract paintings. Some people buy works of art primarily because they are looking for capital appreciation. I don't know what the Medicis would have made of this crass approach, but I can see why a businessman's eyes should light up when he is told that his investment will be worth twice as much a year later.

Many buyers go in for what the Bush administration called 'shock and awe' when it invaded Iraq. Shock because the art is outrageous and awe because of the price tag. Picasso knew the type. So did Andy Warhol, who churned out large paintings of soup cans and other objects – his *Dollar Sign* fetched $4.5 million at an auction in 2005. Today's shockmasters include Brits like Damien Hirst and Tracey Emin. They were 'discovered' by Charles Saatchi, who made a fortune in advertising and then began to trade in works by living artists. He bought their bizarre concoctions for near-nothing in the early 1990s and has since sold for sums up to £12 million.

Hirst, who lived in poverty as a child growing up in Leeds, is best known for his pickled sharks and sheep. I find it hard to see why people should want to have such 'art' in their home but, hey, the man is said to be worth £100 million at the age of 40. Tracey Emin is not yet included in the *Sunday Times* rich list, but she has also done well. There is a story about her which also shows that fame can add value to just about anything. She once stuck posters around London's Spitalfields when she lost her cat Docket. Rabid collectors tore them down and they reportedly changed hands for more than

£500. (Some dealers say they got a bargain.) Charles Saatchi is now betting on people like Zhao, China's pioneer modernist in paint and a hero of Hong Kong salesrooms.

Frank Cohen, a former wallpaper and DIY magnate from Manchester, is another collector with a taste for kitsch modern art. Dubbed the 'Charles Saatchi of the north' by the tabloid media, he is said to have paid £68,000 for an 'installation' which consists of glass boxes containing new bronze casts of excrement covered in 24-carat gold. In America, a jokey painting by Maurizio Cattelan, entitled *The Pope Struck by a Meteorite*, sold for $3 million.

It would be unfair to conclude that all the rich fall for this kind of nonsense. Many are extremely knowledgeable about art and don't seek to shock: they prefer to adorn their homes with paintings by Old Masters and impressionists (the awe is good enough), or with the delightful drawings of talented artists like Ronald Searle and Quentin Blake (Chris Beetles, Europe's biggest dealer in illustrative art, has a worldwide clientele).

Many mega-rich collectors are quite willing to share their treasured possessions, either by lending them for exhibitions or donating them to museums and public galleries in their will. One of the most famous examples is the J. Paul Getty Museum in California. Opened in 1974, it is a large replica of an ancient Roman villa and houses the art collection the oil billionaire had put together over the years; he left many millions to ensure its survival and ability to make new acquisitions. His son, J. Paul Getty II, gave $100 million to various causes, including Britain's National Gallery, during his lifetime. Rockefeller money has financed many fine artists, in the tradition of the Medicis. The Guggenheim family endowed the Museum of Contemporary Art in New York, which bears their name. The world-famous Smithsonian Institution in Washington DC was founded with money left by James Smithson, a British scientist who had never visited the United States.

PARTY TIME

Having acquired and stocked an expensive home, the rich will naturally want to give others a chance to admire their possessions. The obvious way to do that is to throw a party.

Like so much else, parties are not what they were. The Queen can still host one for a thousand guests at Buckingham Palace or Windsor, but few of the rich nowadays have that kind of space. Grand events like charity balls are generally held in five-star hotels. Cocktail parties 'at home' are easy to organise and therefore a popular choice. One should, of course, have flunkeys in white jackets who can handle a tray of drinks without tripping and a personal assistant who will ensure that everything runs smoothly, leaving the host and hostess free to introduce the guests to each other and to explain the works of art if they can. Dinner parties are more serious affairs and are usually planned with meticulous care. One can hire a discreet catering firm, but it is far classier to have one's own chef and immaculately dressed butler.

The main task is to decide who should be invited. In Britain, the Prime Minister is considered a catch but backbench MPs are shunned, especially if they hold left-wing opinions. Bishops and generals are no longer fashionable. Famous actors and TV personalities are acceptable, providing they don't seek to upstage everyone else. Authors are reckoned to be bores. But the greatest ambition of the rich is to capture a senior member of the royal family. The press may mock Charles and Camilla, but they are the next best thing to having the Queen at one's party.

A wealthy American hostess once dared to make fun of the obsession with titles. She invited the crème de la crème of

Newport society to a dinner in honour of Prince de Drago, who had just arrived in the country from far-off Corsica. The 'Prince' turned out to be a bewildered monkey attired in full evening dress. Her guests were not amused.

In Vanderbilt days, it was the custom to place a gift under the napkins of one's guests. There were usually attractive little trinkets, though in at least one reported case, the hostess (a nouveau riche, naturally) felt compelled to provide solid-gold watches. I am told that it can still happen in Arab countries, but in the West people are liable to be acutely embarrassed by obvious bribes. It is, however, essential not to be mean with the food and wine. Champagne should be available before and after dinner, and the wines should be of impeccable vintage.

There are, of course, people who couldn't care less about the 'standards' laid down by the social elite. A super-rich star isn't going to lose any sleep over the lack of invitations from aristocrats and social climbers. Showbiz has its own rules. When Sir Elton John tied the pink knot with his partner, David Furnish, he spent £1 million on an exuberant knees-up for 700 guests in a marquee near his home.

Rich tycoons also like to defy convention. When high-street billionaire Philip Green decided to give a bash for his 50th birthday, he flew 200 chums to Cyprus and greeted them dressed as the Emperor Nero. The event was reported to have cost him £5 million. His best friend and business associate, Richard Caring, hosted a three-day charity extravaganza in St Petersburg and arranged for each of his guests to be measured up for appropriate Russian costumes.

Another flamboyant billionaire, Sol Kerzner, invited 300 guests to his 70th birthday party at the Sporting Club in Monte Carlo. (Officially his glamorous 35-year-old wife did so, but everyone knew who was picking up the tab.)

Kerzner, a former boxing champion, made his first fortune

in South Africa's hotel trade. During the years of apartheid he had the clever idea of building a resort, Sun City, in one of the independent black states, where wealthy whites could gamble and enjoy other pastimes frowned upon by the regime in Pretoria. It was a huge success. He has since made many more millions by opening casino resorts in other countries, notably the Bahamas.

His birthday party was spectacular. Liza Minelli, Shirley Bassey and Natalie Cole respectively belted out hits like 'New York, New York', 'Hey Big Spender' and 'This Will Be (An Everlasting Love)'. A personal video message was beamed in from Nelson Mandela.

Vikram Chatwal, a wealthy Indian hotelier, did even better. When he married a model and actress, Priya Sachdev, his celebration lasted ten days and was spread across three cities. More than 600 guests from 26 countries, including Bill Clinton, were ferried around on chartered jets. The odyssey finally took them to New Delhi, where Vikram climbed on a white horse and led a half-mile procession to the Taj Mahal hotel, where he was greeted by the bride's family in a traditional welcoming ceremony attended by India's Prime Minister.

The Chatwals could well afford such lavish hospitality. His father had founded the Bombay Palace restaurants and the Hampshire Hotels and Resorts chain. In New York, Vikram had long been known as a playboy, and Dad was delighted when he announced that he was ready to settle down with a nice Indian girl. 'It was a big deal for them', Priya told the media.

Britain's royals also know how to put on an impressive show – indeed, they still do it better than anyone else. Visiting heads of state can expect to be entertained in regal style, and the Queen hosts an annual garden party for her subjects at Buckingham Palace. But weddings, nowadays, are often low-key affairs. This was certainly the case when Prince Charles married his long-time mistress, Camilla Parker-Bowles. It will no doubt be different when Prince William eventually walks down the aisle at Westminster Abbey.

CHAPTER 12

THE TOYS OF THE RICH

Getting around in style is as important to the rich as having the right place to live. For centuries, the answer was the carriage – from kings in their golden coaches to country squires in their elegant gigs, men of wealth displayed their standing by the splendour of their equipage. They had a bumpy ride until good springs were first used in the mid-18th century, but they were an imposing sight as they splashed through the mud with their teams of fine horses.

In the latter part of the 19th century, private railroad cars became an equally important status symbol. Many of them looked like miniature palaces with gilded ceilings, expensive French furniture and even pianos. They can still be found in India, but are no longer used by the maharajahs who once owned them – most have become part of the tourist trade. (I once had an enjoyable week's journey through Rajasthan in the aptly named 'Palace on Wheels', which consists of a number of such cars linked together.)

When the motor car appeared on the scene, some of the rich were sceptical, and some downright hostile, but the more daring gave the new conveyance an enthusiastic welcome. By the 1920s, a Rolls Royce had become almost de rigueur. The super-rich, eager to outdo each other, ordered models which incorporated some of the features of the railroad car. Rolls Royce still points with pride to some of its creations, like the sumptuous drawing-room-on-wheels it built for a French millionaire in 1927: the upholstery was woven by Aubusson and the ceiling was painted with rococo cupids.

Cupids are out of fashion but the Rolls is not – it is still one of the first things many people buy when they have made serious money. Some of the mega-rich rulers of Middle East countries have a fleet of them: the Sultan of Brunei, for example, is reputed to own more than 300.

Showbiz celebrities may also be provided with a stretch limo, complete with a bar and satellite TV, but this is considered to be rather vulgar. Many prefer to be seen in a Ferrari or Maserati, because they want to convey a youthful image. In car-mad California, there are people with so many of these expensive toys that they find it hard to make up their minds which one to wheel out for the day.

If they have homes in another part of the country, or abroad, the rich will naturally keep cars in all of them. Some enjoy driving, but if they are invited to an important social event they must be conveyed there by a well-dressed and deferential chauffeur. Getting stuck in traffic can be avoided by acquiring a helicopter. There is plainly much to be said for flitting over roads and motorways on the way to and from one's estate or making a grand entrance at a bash. In London, the Battersea Heliport is the metropolitan epicentre; hang out there and you are bound to bump into one of the heli-crowd. At Ascot, each summer, so many choppers are parked in the fields that, as the society magazine *Tatler* has noted, they 'look as if they have been infested by a plague of great metallic grasshoppers'.

For longer trips, a private plane is widely regarded as

essential. It saves all that airport hassle that the rest of us have to put up with. America has by far the largest number, which isn't surprising when you consider the size and affluence of the country, but they are used just about everywhere. Oil-rich plutocrats have a penchant for large jets, like the Boeing 767, which can be converted for personal use. They are the modern equivalent of the golden coach or railroad car, with the kind of luxurious amenities we can only dream about. Corporate tycoons generally prefer a sleek Gulfstream jet – paid for and maintained at the company's expense.

Yachts are another favourite toy of the rich. At one time, yachting was a largely aristocratic pursuit, involving real sailing. Only a small number of self-made millionaires joined in. One was the super-rich American financier, J.P. Morgan, who used to entertain society ladies on his *Sea Wolf*. Asked by a guest how much a boat like this cost, he famously replied: 'If you have to ask, you can't afford it.'

Even Morgan would be amazed if he could see some of today's seductive playthings. Size in the world of super-yachts is an important measure of virility, as befits the toys of men with egos to match their bank balance. In the 1960s, an 80-foot yacht was big. These days, 'big' is anything from 180 to over 400 feet.

One of the early trendsetters was the legendary Greek shipping mogul, Aristotle Onassis. His nautical behemoth, the *Christina*, was like a floating billboard proclaiming: 'I've made it!' Old Money families were appalled by his determined ostentation and sniggered at his vulgarity (he had the cocktail bar stools made of elephants' foreskins) but the nouveau riche were awed and envious. The guest list also impressed them. Winston Churchill was often photographed on deck, smoking a cigar. John and Jackie Kennedy were among the many other celebrities who enjoyed his lavish hospitality – Jackie, of course, later became Mrs Onassis.

By the 1980s, the traditional Mediterranean playgrounds were chock-a-block with luxurious yachts. The Greek islands were also part of the social circuit. But many owners spent only two or three weeks a year on their boats, and some rarely left their moorings. ('I get seasick', one told me.)

One of the largest boats was owned by Sir Donald Gosling. A cheerful cockney, he had served in the Navy as an able seaman during the Second World War. When the war ended, he and a partner bought a lot of bombsites and started what eventually became National Car Parks. He later used his huge wealth to acquire a 161-foot boat, which he called *Brave Goose*.

When I first met him, in the South of France, he had added another outsize yacht, the *Leander*. He told me how proud he was that admirals and royals were regular guests and that he had become an honorary captain in the Navy.

I also went on several cruises along the coast with Sir Nigel Broackes, the founder of Trafalgar House – a conglomerate that owned Cunard. I accompanied him when he bought a magnificent new toy, the *Mikado*. It was fast and equipped with all the latest gadgets – sails hidden in three masts unfurled electronically. There was a fireplace in the drawing room and a carpet that whisked away at the touch of a button to reveal a dance floor. Nigel, alas, had only a few years more to live.

Another tycoon who proudly showed me around his toy was Robert Maxwell. This was before the world – and I – discovered that he was a crook. Maxwell had acquired a publishing company I headed at the time and I was on holiday in Cannes when he invited me to dinner. 'Where are you?' I asked. 'In Sardinia', he said. 'Bob', I pointed out, 'it is 2 pm here and I don't see how I can possibly get to Sardinia by 7 pm.'

'No problem', he replied. 'I'll send my plane to get you.'

This turned out to be a Gulfstream jet, which I boarded at the airport in Nice. I was the only passenger and a glamorous attendant kept offering me Dom Pérignon champagne, which I found hard to resist. Dinner on board the *Lady Ghislaine* (named after one of his daughters) was pleasant and I stayed overnight. Early the next morning – this was about 6 am – we had breakfast and Maxwell said that he was returning to London in the Gulfstream and wanted me to go with him. When we arrived at Heathrow, his helicopter was waiting and we soon landed on the pad of his office building in the City. I was, of course, impressed by this flamboyant display of wealth (all paid for by the business empire he had created), but my relationship with Bob ended long before he was found floating in the sea, dead, after he had spent a few days on the yacht 'recovering from a cold'. The cause of his death remains a mystery – did he jump or was he pushed? I am inclined to believe that it was suicide, because he was in such deep financial trouble that he would almost certainly have been sent to jail.

Many of today's mega-yachts have everything a billionaire could want: swimming pools, king-sized canopied state rooms with mirrored ceilings, speedboats and jet skis, discos, cinemas, helipads, satellite communications systems, or even operating theatres. A new fad, still in its infancy, is a private submarine. Paul Allen, co-founder with Bill Gates of Micro-soft, owns a bright yellow submarine capable of taking ten passengers. The craft is said to be docked, James-Bond style, in his 416-foot yacht.

All this could easily cost $200 million – and that's not counting the astronomical expense of the crew, flunkeys, repairs, fuel, insurance and mooring fees. Some of the outlay can be covered by chartering, but it still adds up to a vast commitment.

When the weather turns chilly, many super-yachts are

dispatched to the warmer climate of the Caribbean. But there is a problem – some are so big that their very size rules out docking at most marinas. Coastal resorts around the world are racing to build or retrofit their facilities to accommodate them.

Sir Richard Branson and other entrepreneurs are planning to offer what they claim will be the ultimate travel experience for the rich – a space tour. They won't be the first. In 2005, a wealthy American, Greg Olsen, was the third millionaire to pay around $20 million to US firm Space Adventures to go into space. He had to undergo two years of rigorous training before taking the round-trip to the International Space Station in a small Soyuz capsule. Branson's venture, Virgin Galactic, is offering a less ambitious alternative. It aims to send paying passengers on sub-orbital flights. A spokesman said early in 2006 that 157 people had already put down deposits totalling more than $12 million. A spaceport is being built in New Mexico and operations are scheduled to start in 2008. Meanwhile, Space Adventures has commissioned a specially designed Russian spacecraft, which should also be ready that year, and is building a $265 million spaceport in the United Arab Emirates.

THE SPORT OF KINGS – AND TYCOONS

Not everyone, of course, wants to have a yacht or to be a space traveller. Many people prefer to stay on terra firma.

A popular pastime is the ownership of capricious horses. Earlier generations used them for transport; today's owners are more likely to be interested in winning races, which most of these splendid creatures stubbornly refuse to do. I have yet to meet a rich man who does not complain, often at length, about the expense and the disappointments involved in the 'sport of kings', but when one enquires why they persist, they seem amazed that anyone should ask such a foolish question. One owns a horse because it is the thing to do and, besides, it may one day be first past the post and make a lot of money.

Racing was originally the almost exclusive domain of European aristocrats. The situation is entirely different today. The Queen still maintains an impressive racing stable, but most owners are wealthy tycoons and people who are coyly described in some magazines as 'foreign gentlemen' – sheikhs and other rulers of oil-rich states. In America, many successful stables are owned by entrepreneurs who have made millions and who see it as an effective way of gaining status among the more established families of the upper class. The Kentucky Derby and other premier races are major social events.

The usual methods of acquiring a racehorse are to buy a yearling at an auction. Prices vary. When I last went to a Newmarket sale, one filly went for £825,000 and a colt for £800,000. But that's only the start: you also have to pay for feeding, stabling, training and, in due course, entering your horse in a race.

Some people try to make a business out of the sport. One British tycoon set up a stable of 120 horses with the specific aim of making a profit from prizes. His venture succeeded in that he regularly won over 100 races a year, but the prize money involved was never enough and he eventually gave up. Other entrepreneurs use a different approach: they are mainly concerned with breeding stallions. To raise a thoroughbred champion is the dream of thousands around the world. Every time a fuzzy, wide-eyed and gawky foal hits the ground, each breeder hopes that this will be a king of racing. But only a third make it to the racetrack and the chances of winning one of the famous events are slim. All kinds of methods are used to narrow the field, including computer technology, but it's hard to project the idiosyncrasies of biology or tabulate the courage in a horse's heart.

A champion can make his owner a fortune in prizes and stud fees. Most of the rich, though, don't think in terms of business. They like gambling, and they like the idea of proudly showing off a winner bearing their very own colours in a major race. In Britain, the big events are the Derby, the Grand National, Goodwood, and Ascot. Everyone wants to win the Derby, but Ascot is the main social occasion. Each day's racing opens with a royal procession down the middle of the course. The Queen and Prince Philip are always in the front carriage; men doff their hats as they pass by. To get into the Royal Enclosure one has to secure permission from Her Majesty's representative. Until the early 1960s people who had been through the divorce courts were banned; so were journalists and members of other unsuitable trades. The rules have been relaxed, but men are still expected to wear morning dress and a grey topper. Women have an opportunity to display the latest creations of fashion designers. Some go to extraordinary lengths to get attention. Hats, in particular, tend to be remarkable concoctions, ranging from over the top to totally outrageous.

In America, the Kentucky Derby is a must, and the rich also like to be seen at the leading racetracks of New York, Florida and Los Angeles. In Australia, the biggest annual event is the Melbourne Cup – their version of Ascot.

I have never had a desire to own a racehorse but I enjoy riding. Give me a friendly, obedient mare or stallion that will trot through what is left of the English countryside and I am quite content. I have also been to dude ranches in the US where one can have a great time on horseback for what a billionaire would regard as small change. He or she may have a vast spread, and hundreds of horses, but you don't *have* to be rich to indulge in one of the most agreeable recreations.

YOUR CLUB OR MINE?

There are many other pastimes which attract less attention. I once met a multi-millionaire who had a huge train set in his mansion and often invited other tycoons to play with it. He would dress up in a stationmaster's uniform and maintain control by pressing hidden buttons. The late Malcolm Forbes, the billionaire magazine publisher, accumulated one of the world's largest collections of toy soldiers. He and his friends would, apparently, stage great mock battles between the French and the British armies. Hugh Hefner liked to challenge guests like me to combat on one of his many pinball machines. Richard Branson is fond of hot air balloons.

By far the most popular hobby is golf. Like riding, it doesn't necessarily require great wealth – the equipment isn't expensive and many courses are open to the public. But membership of an exclusive club is another matter. Many are controlled by Old Money snobs who seek to keep out the newly rich. High fees don't deter them, so membership committees tend to resort to more subtle means. Applicants are put on long waiting lists and when they finally reach the end of the queue they may find themselves blackballed.

The obvious solution for a rejected tycoon is to start or buy his own club. Some have done just that. It costs a fortune but you get to make the rules, which is even better for the ego than gobbling up a rival corporation.

For many players, golf is more than a game. It is also about politics and business. Many lucrative deals have been initiated between holes. Some investment bankers, stockbrokers and company chairmen seem to do little else – their job is to go out on the course and nail wealthy customers.

LICENCE TO KILL

The same is often true of another favourite activity – shooting. Not, I hasten to point out, each other (though the temptation may be there and accidents *will* happen), but animals. Guns are among the most treasured toys of the rich.

When Britain still had an empire, the nobility would go to Asia to hunt tigers and to Africa to shoot lions and other wildlife. Their skills frequently left much to be desired but they made up in sheer volume of carnage what they lacked in fitness.

The Maharajahs of India would provide their guests with docile elephants, equipped with comfortable seating, so that they could kill from a lofty distance. They also had trackers who could locate any tiger who had merely been wounded. In Africa, the earls and viscounts were accompanied by professional white hunters who knew how to keep them out of trouble when they were confronted by predators. Many nobles had the heads of lions stuffed and shipped home, where they were proudly displayed in the drawing room or library.

The nouveau riche were so impressed that they, too, felt the need to gun down exotic creatures. In America, buffalo hunting became a fashionable sport. A predictable result of all this relentless pursuit of wildlife was that many species eventually became harder to find – indeed, some were thought likely to become extinct if the slaughter continued. The government of India, no longer willing to let Maharajahs and the British have their way, decided that tigers had to be protected, and was given strong support by international organisations like the World Wildlife Fund. In Africa, countries like Kenya imposed a ban on hunting. Today the rich have to do their shooting elsewhere.

In Britain this mainly means going after pheasants, grouse, and other birds. Many country estates have turned it into a lucrative business – the potential victims are encouraged to breed before being blasted out of the sky by affluent people who are more than willing to pay the hefty fees charged for the privilege.

Animal rights activists have become increasingly vocal, and sometimes violent, in their opposition. They have already succeeded in getting the Labour government to ban fox hunting and are determined to stamp out other pastimes they associate with the rich. Many genuinely care about animals, but there are also many who see it as part of the class war. The irony is that a number will quite happily buy meat in supermarkets. Cows are 'steaks' or 'Sunday roasts'. Pigs are 'ham' or 'pork'. A chicken or lamb is not an animal but Sunday *lunch*.

This attitude is even more true of fish. One of my office colleagues expressed dismay when I wrote an article in *High Life* about game fishing – one of the sports which the rich can still indulge in without retribution. How, she said, could I approve of something that was so cruel? I replied that, on the few occasions I had done it, I had worked bloody hard to catch my quarry – half an hour or more strapped in a chair on a rocking boat, fighting a smart game fish, was very different from buying a neatly wrapped slice in Tesco or Sainsbury. I hadn't used a gun, and it had been given a much better chance of getting away than it would have been by the owners of fishing fleets equipped with modern technology. If she was so concerned about the welfare of fish, then the obvious solution was to become a vegetarian.

HIGH ROLLERS

When they are not busy shooting or fishing, many rich people like to indulge in another diversion – playing for big stakes in a casino.

There is nothing new about this, but much has changed in recent decades. The European aristocrats who used to dominate casino gambling have been largely replaced by the nouveau riche, who have deeper pockets. London's discreet private clubs attract affluent players from all over the world, especially the Middle East. The late Kerry Packer, an Australian media billionaire, was a renowned high roller: he would often win or lose as much as £1 million in one evening. In 2005, parliament passed a Gambling Act which will allow new casinos across the country; the first are expected to open in 2008.

Monaco also remains popular, but the most famous place today is that 24-hour American city of fantasy, Las Vegas. It is artificial, vulgar and greedy, a neon playground which bombards the senses with a maelstrom of sights and sounds. The casinos are vast. Walking into one of them for the first time is a stunning experience – you are overwhelmed by a cacophony of clicking, clacking, buzzing, and the 'come on' shouts of a thousand optimistic players. Banks of slot machines blink their multi-coloured eyes; bells and flashing lights announce a win.

Serious players view the small stuff with disdain. They are after the big bucks. If they are rich, and willing to risk some of their millions, the casino will treat them like royalty. (One manager told me that they are known as 'whales' because they make big waves; it seems a more apt description.) Everything is free, from private planes and fancy limos to opulent suites and glamorous 'escorts'.

On my last visit to this human zoo, I talked to a whale from New York. He said that he liked to gamble because it gave him the same thrill he got when he first started his company. 'It isn't the money', he insisted. 'I've got plenty. It's the challenge. I've always been a very competitive person. I like to get the best of everything and anybody I can get the best of. When I went into business on my own, I was often close to disaster. One bad deal could have finished me. I worried a lot at the time but, you know, it was the most exciting time of my life. Today the company is very successful and I have good people who are perfectly capable of running it. You can't experience the thrill of winning if there's no chance of losing. So I come here twice a year.'

Las Vegas has many rivals, notably Atlantic City and the large casinos built on Indian reservations, but there's nothing quite like this bizarre oasis in the Nevada desert. It's one of those places that one should aim to see at least once, even if one isn't a whale.

THE FASHION GAME

Although they dress up for occasions like Ascot, men are generally less interested in fashion than women. A surprisingly large number of people who could well afford to pay a good tailor make do with clothes bought off the rack. Many say that they are too busy to find time for something as frivolous as fashion, but there is often another reason. The business world still tends to equate conservative dress with financial responsibility, and they don't want to be thought irresponsible. They may take a chance at weekends or on holiday, but seldom in everyday life. Even dinner jackets are dull.

There are, of course, exceptions. Super-rich men like Bill Gates, Steve Jobs and Sir Richard Branson don't give a fig for convention, judging by the way they dress in public. But they also show little, if any, inclination to look like the young male models in magazines. Most wealthy entrepreneurs prefer to leave that sort of exhibitionism to rock stars and other show-biz celebrities.

Female executives generally try to look smart rather than sexy. Many wear suits because they don't want to stand out.

The wives of the rich tend to be more adventurous. As many see it, they are a walking advertisement for their husband's affluence and simply cannot be expected to shop at Marks & Spencer. It is their patronage which makes the big money for top designers and for fashion magazines like *Vogue*. They don't care about the cost but will not forgive duplication: the worst that can happen, in their eyes, is to go to a party and find that someone else is wearing the same dress.

I am always amazed by the coverage of fashion shows in the media. It is hard to believe that women actually *buy* the absurd creations displayed by stick-thin models as they sashay down the catwalk. But they obviously do. They also pay fancy prices for hats, shoes, handbags and jewellery.

A DIAMOND'S BEST FRIEND

What makes one rich woman really different from another (or so many tend to think) is the quantity and quality of her jewels. Secretaries and suburban housewives with diamonds the size of a pinhead are held in amused contempt – anything less than a 3-carat stone doesn't begin to rate. The ideal is a flawless gem which is big enough to draw envious glances. The late Richard Burton had the right idea when he presented Elizabeth Taylor with a large pear-shaped diamond that cost him more than a million dollars. If a mere actor can do it, thousands of women must have told themselves, a property developer or shipping tycoon should be able to do the same. (Oil-rich Arabs certainly can. One bought a beautiful heart-shaped diamond of 62 carats from a renowned New York dealer. He subsequently returned it as part of a down payment for $2 million worth of other jewellery, explaining that he really needed four big diamonds exactly alike, one for each of his wives.)

An engagement ring is usually reckoned to be the first rung on the ladder, but many attractive women start a lot earlier than that. A rich man is expected to hand out baubles from the moment he makes an advance. A diamond bracelet can greatly help his cause. A mistress will try to persuade him to add other gifts as the affair progresses; a wife will *insist* on generous treatment. Expensive jewellery can compensate for many things, including neglect. ('You are always working.') Quarrels, birthdays, anniversaries and Christmas provide suitable excuses for the handing over of diamond earrings, emerald necklaces and other trinkets. Designers are constantly encouraged to explore fresh and exotic avenues, but true snobs hanker after jewellery with an interesting history – a necklace that once belonged to Marie-Antoinette makes a much better conversation piece than one which has just emerged from the workshop.

When the Greek shipping billionaire Aristotle Onassis married the widow of President Kennedy, Jackie, he gave her jewelled earrings depicting Apollo 11's visit to the moon, featuring a 40-carat diamond. They had a sapphire-studded earth to clip on her ears, with a moon decorated with rubies hanging from a chain, and a miniature Apollo ship attached to a thin gold thread to circle the earth and drop to the moon. To get all this on a delicate lady's lobes, her ears would have to be as big as a donkey's. But Jackie managed it. For a Christmas present, he gave her not one diamond but a whole diamond mine.

Wealthy women can, of course, afford to buy their own status symbols. An essential item is a luxury watch – one with lots of diamonds. The seriously rich have a *wardrobe* of glitzy watches for every occasion. The brand name is important but what really counts is exclusivity. How about a 'limited edition' timepiece from Chanel, for a mere $130,000? Or, perhaps, a 'unique' Blancpain Quattro from Cortina? Housed in a sapphire black platinum case with 36 baguette-cut diamonds totalling 6.9 carats, it is priced at $273,000.

If you think that's expensive, consider what old watches are sold for at auctions. One piece by Piguet & Mylath, made in 1820, went for $349,000. A 1933 watch from Patek Philippe fetched $11 million, while the company's 1939 'World Time' wristwatch brought $4 million.

The fashion industry has made strenuous efforts, over the years, to convince men that they should also buy diamond rings, bracelets and flashy cufflinks. It has had considerable success with people in showbiz and even in sport – David Beckham is renowned for his love of bling. But business tycoons have been reluctant to go along. They tend to associate jewellery with shady characters, car salesmen and what many still coyly refer to as the gay community. An elegant watch from Rolex or Cartier is acceptable; a chunky gold bracelet is not.

Cellini in New York will sell you a 'Caliber RM 008-V2 Tourbillon Split Seconds Chronograph' in titanium, white gold, pink gold, or platinum. (Ideal for a tycoon whose time is precious.) It is water-resistant to 50 metres, so you don't have to take it off if you fancy a spot of diving. Prices start at $455,000.

There is also a brisk trade in vintage watches. A gold Rolex given as a birthday present to JFK by Marilyn Monroe, inscribed 'Jack, with love as always Marilyn, May 29th 1962' was sold for $100,000 at auction. (Perfect if your name is Jack.)

Jewellery stores say that wealthy women often buy trinkets for their husbands or toyboy lovers. I would rather have a Ferrari, but my wife says that I am too old for life in the fast lane.

CHAPTER 13

GIVE AND TAKE

Neiman Marcus, the famous Texas department store for the rich, publishes an annual Christmas catalogue with a bizarre choice of gifts. Here are some of the items featured in recent years:

An 18-carat gold, jewel-studded teddy bear holding a pocket watch that chimes every hour

A five-foot-high acrylic aquarium shaped like an elephant

A levitating aluminium and wood sculpture that sits on an invisible magnetic wave hovering in the air indefinitely

A Zeppelin airship

Your own rideable railroad system with a locomotive, cars, stations and 1,000 feet of track

A midget submarine

A life-size portable replica of your spouse, relative or

friend, 'programmed to laugh for as long as you like at your jokes or say yes in any language you choose at the touch of a button'.

It's hard to believe that people actually spend big money on such outrageous stuff, and that anyone would say: 'Oh, great, a Zeppelin. Just what I've always wanted.' But hey – this is America.

My Old Money friends assure me that *they* would never give vulgar presents and that they would be offended if someone else did so. Only the nouveau riche, they insist, would contemplate such foolishness.

It is certainly important to do one's homework. A basic mistake is to assume that others share our tastes. We have all been at the receiving end of gifts that we absolutely hated. The rich are no different.

The wealthy owner of a British company once told me that a supplier sent him what he no doubt thought was a hilarious Christmas present: an Executive Problem Solver. It consisted of a small scaffold complete with a noose. The supplier had, alas, neglected to find out if his business partner had a sense of humour. He didn't. As far as he was concerned, it was a childish and insulting gesture. He promptly cancelled the contract.

Most of us are flattered by evidence that people have taken the trouble to establish what will give genuine pleasure. Discreet enquiries will usually tell you all you need to know. *Who's Who* is also a helpful guide to the interests of the rich and famous.

For Old Money, grace and style is every bit as important as substance. New Money people may be more interested in novelty but they, too, appreciate thoughtfulness. Some of my rich friends are avid collectors. One has more than a dozen vintage cars; another is proud of his collection of musical instruments, including four pianos and a Swiss alpenhorn. I have met multi-millionaires who are fond of medieval armour and busts of great men like Julius Caesar, Napoleon and Churchill. One basic rule applies to all: gifts should always be a personal expression of friendship and esteem.

In the corporate world, gift-giving often has a different motive – to gain commercial favours. This has long been a controversial aspect. Many companies have developed their own policy. Some ban the receipt of any item. Others forbid the acceptance of anything over a specified value. It makes sense, but can create problems if one is doing business in countries where generosity is regarded as essential to a good reputation. The Arabs, for example, give much and expect to be treated equally well. They have no respect for rich people who don't spend freely, and find it hard to understand why so many Westerners are skinflints.

When Jimmy Carter was President of the United States, he and his wife Rosalynn visited a camel market during a trip to Egypt. The wealthy owner was so honoured that he presented the couple with two silver daggers, several whips, and a six-year-old camel with a pink ribbon around its neck. He was barely prevented from slaughtering a sheep at their feet in a traditional gesture of welcome. An embarrassed Carter rebuked the American embassy for not briefing him properly on Arab customs so he could provide a gift of his own.

Queen Elizabeth II has been at the receiving end of more strange presents than any other Western head of state. They have included totem poles, snow shoes, ice-picks, spears, talking drums, fly-whisks, swords, a gold replica of Karachi Town Hall, a large statue of a bucking bronco, a three-foot pottery vase, a bronze cauldron, baby elephants, bears, crocodiles, boa constrictors and turtles. She has always managed to look grateful for the largesse, though privately she has found much of it puzzling. Refusal, of course, was out of the question.

The exotic livestock has usually ended up in London Zoo. The totem poles and many other objects have been made available to museums on permanent loan – the polite fiction being maintained that if Her Majesty had a sudden urge to make use of, say, her ceremonial sword from Kyoto, the curator would instantly remove it from its glass case and send it round by special messenger. The Palace has also kept a record of gifts so that they can be whisked into a prominent position if a donor comes to stay.

The Foreign Office nowadays offers discreet advice to hosts but there is no guarantee that it will be taken. Officials have let it be known that the Queen will not accept expensive presents from private persons with whom she is not acquainted, but gifts from organisations and foreign dignitaries are less easily stopped. It would certainly be ill-mannered to reject the diamond-studded insignia of noble rank which many countries like to bestow on distinguished visitors. (The Queen, incidentally, has the final say over whether her subjects should be allowed to wear such gifts in public when they get back home. This dates back to the time of the first Queen Elizabeth, who got so annoyed by the lavish distinctions conferred on her courtiers by scheming foreigners that she decreed: 'They are my dogs and they shall wear *my* collars.' British citizens still need written permission from the monarch.)

Much thought has been given over the years to the matter of reciprocity. Should the royals hand out items that could be said to represent the British way of life – a prime Scottish bull, a herd of Welsh sheep, an English horse, or perhaps a gold replica of Windsor Castle? The standard practice has been to play it safe by giving an engraved silver tray or bowl, plus a signed photograph in an elegant frame. The Queen may also bestow honorary knighthoods, if the government agrees, but the insignia is far from grand. It may strike some of the recipients as miserly (the Queen is super-rich and Britain is a prosperous country), but that is the way we do these things in the 21st century, and it's certainly more classy than President George Bush's habit of presenting world leaders with cowboy boots.

British ministers are expected to adhere to a strict code, at home and abroad. Nothing, but nothing, must be allowed to give the impression that they can be bribed. Older readers may recall the Tale of the Silver Coffee Pot, which made headlines when a previous Labour government was in power. It had been given to Tony Crosland, then a cabinet minister, after he had opened a new building constructed by a man called Poulson. Gifts of this kind were commonplace at the time, and Crosland wrote the usual letter of appreciation. 'I am', he said, 'most grateful for the very beautiful coffee pot you so kindly gave me and my wife. I shall treasure it in memory of a very beautiful building.' What he didn't know was that Poulson was busy bribing all sorts of local officials and would before long find himself in prison. When he was exposed, and sentenced, Crosland was besieged by reporters. 'I don't care tuppence for that dammed pot', he protested. 'It's been lying in the cupboard for seven years with a lot of other lunatic things and has never been used. All I want to do is to get rid of the bloody thing.'

The affair blew over but led to the introduction of tighter rules. Today every minister is well aware that any breach of the code can spell the end of a promising career. Gifts with any serious value must always be handed over to a civil service aide and will not be seen again – unless, as sometimes happens, he or she is supplied with the same item from the government pool ahead of an official visit to a country.

THE EYE OF THE NEEDLE

When Tony Blair went to see the new Pope at the Vatican, he gave him two CDs of music by the German pontiff's favourite composer, Mozart. In return he got Benedict's blessing – a fair exchange.

Popes have not always been so easy to please. For many centuries they expected visitors to arrive with lavish presents.

Jesus famously said that it is 'easier for a camel to go through the eye of a needle than for a rich man to enter the Kingdom of God'. His Catholic vicars not only lived in regal splendour but assured rich men that the eye could be conveniently widened if the right price was paid.

Pope Leo X had 683 courtiers and servants, including a court composer, several jesters and a keeper of the elephants. He kept his own permanent orchestra and theatre company, and when he went on one of his frequent hunting expeditions he was accompanied by 200 riders, including cardinals, musicians and comedians. To pay for it all, he pushed the sale of benefices and indulgences to such extremes that it provoked Luther's revolt and the Reformation. He appointed a number of cardinals, from whom he extorted a great deal of money, and created and sold no fewer than 1,200 new offices.

The Vatican is still one of the most magnificent edifices on earth, and the Pope's Summer Palace (complete with swimming pool) is the envy of many multi-millionaires. But pontiffs no longer seek to accumulate personal wealth. Like his more recent predecessors, Benedict gets no salary and certainly cannot be called rich.

The greatest worry of Vatican officials is that any new man will (like Christ) take an 'irresponsible' view of money. There have been some notable examples of papal generosity: they still recall with horror a previous Pope Benedict's custom of

171

keeping large sums in his suite and handing them freely to any priest who came to him with a tale of woe. In the 1970s, Pope Jean Paul I acknowledged the contradiction between the ideal of poverty preached by the Saviour and the wealth of the Holy See. He told an audience in St Peter's: 'The Church must be poor and appear to be poor.' His officials dismissed the argument as 'moral simplicity' and managed to persuade him that the Vatican couldn't afford to give away its assets.

The main source of income, apart from bequests and dividends from investments, is 'Peter's Pence' – money given by the world's Catholics. A website says that it can be sent directly to His Holiness by post, credit card or online. Most contributions, however, are collected locally. They vary considerably according to the size of the diocese, the wealth and religious zeal of the inhabitants, and the efficiency of its clergy. Donations are also influenced by the charisma of the reigning pontiff and the view people take of his needs. In the 19th century, parish priests in many European countries distributed to the faithful picture cards, depicting the Pope lying on a bed of straw in a dark dungeon, to corroborate the legend that he was a prisoner of the wicked Italians and reduced to extreme poverty. Money poured in. If they tried such a ploy today, the Vatican would be besieged by TV camera crews and reporters determined to expose the whole thing as a diabolical fake.

The Church of England's wealth is less obvious and few people worry about the lifestyle of the Archbishop of Canterbury. A body called the Church Commissioners controls assets estimated at £4.3 billion. They include large tracts of land – 120,000 acres in rural areas alone – and investments in offices, shopping centres, industrial estates and the stock market. Millions are donated each year by the 'man in the pew', and by some rich people, but the Commissioners say that the amount of money at their disposal is inadequate. Churches have to be repaired and salaries have to be paid. Most clergymen earn less than skilled workers; in today's materialistic terms they are indeed poor and seen to be poor.

A major concern for Church of England officials is that church attendances across the country are in decline. In many parts of Britain, more people go to mosques than to Christian places of worship. Many of us, it seems, also prefer to give financial support to other religious organisations. This isn't a new trend: it began in the 1960s when Indian gurus attracted celebrities like the Beatles.

One of the first on the scene was the Maharishi Mahesh Yogi, who converted thousands of people to his doctrine of Spiritual Regeneration. The Beatles soon defected, but the Maharishi's grandly named 'World Government' continued to recruit followers. It grew so rich that it was able to buy two hotels near Lake Lucerne, where it established its international headquarters, and several expensive properties in America and Britain, including Mentmore Towers, a Victorian mansion in Buckinghamshire formerly owned by the Rothschild family. One of its many ventures is a Transcendental Meditation Programme for Business.

Another prominent guru was Bhagwan ('Lord God') Shree Rajnesh, who claimed that his movement was 'the route to the preservation of the human race'. At its peak, it had 200,000 members and 600 centres around the world and its founder was a multi-millionaire who lived in luxury: his toys included a collection of 27 Rolls Royces given to him by his disciples. When he died in 1990, at the age of 59, it was widely rumoured that he had been poisoned by the CIA.

There are many groups which make fanciful promises and are plainly run by charlatans. It's easy to dismiss people who fall for them as gullible fools, but faith is such a personal

173

matter, and gives comfort to so many, that we should not judge them too harshly. As the Pope and the Archbishop of Canterbury would no doubt wish to stress, we are all entitled to our own opinion and it's up to individuals to decide what to do with their money.

CHAPTER 14

THE GREATEST
APHRODISIAC?

Countless paperback novels have encouraged the view that
the rich lead more interesting sex lives than the rest of us.
One does not *have* to be wealthy to indulge in sexual games-
manship, but it helps. A rich man can afford to set up
mistresses in cosy apartments; a rich woman has the means
to buy the attention of handsome lovers. Money is a great
aphrodisiac. So, of course, is power. Put the two together and
you have a combination which many find irresistible.

Much has been written about the alleged antics of Hollywood film moguls. Looks had nothing to do with their sex
appeal – some of them were downright ugly. Money and
power was (and is) everything. The same is true of others
who are able to promote the careers of ambitious people.
Hugh Hefner, who has been to bed with more women than
Casanova, helped his girlfriends by featuring them in his
magazine and introducing them to producers. I doubt if they
would have been as eager to please him if he had been a
struggling insurance salesman.

Captains of industry may have many advantages. They can,
and do, invest in films and stage plays on condition that their

mistresses are given leading roles. They can, and do, help them to climb the corporate ladder. They can, and do, offer women the opportunity to live in idle luxury. They can, and do, divorce wives who have been with them through the rough years.

The divorce rate among the rich is comparatively high because they tend to be more restless, more easily bored, more tempted to change for the sake of change. They find it easy to convince themselves that a new partner will provide greater happiness. It doesn't always work out like that, of course, but they can afford to experiment.

Self-made tycoons are notoriously vulnerable. They tend to marry early, often choosing a dull but supportive woman who will cook their meals, bring up their children, listen to their plans, and applaud their ambition. Sex soon becomes a once-a-week chore because they are too tired, or too preoccupied with business matters, to perform more frequently. Some wives take lovers, but it's a risky game because their would-be tycoon, though unwilling to play the part of ardent stud, fiercely resents the idea that his wife may find another man more appealing. It undermines his self-confidence.

The moment of danger arrives when he has climbed to the top of whatever hill he has had his eyes on. He can relax and turn his attention to the good things in life. Loyalty is no longer the main consideration when he looks at a woman. His wife, worn out by years of caring for him and his brood, suddenly seems intolerably drab. She knows all his faults (which is irritating) and she is a poor advertisement for a successful man.

It is at this point that he is liable to fall heavily for a glamorous young woman. She openly admires his success (which is gratifying), refrains from criticism (which is comforting), and revives his interest in sex. Friends comment on her beauty and he basks in the praise of his new conquest. Because he is vain and knows next to nothing about the wiles of women, he finds it easy to believe that she is interested in his finer human qualities and prowess in bed, rather than in his money.

In the early stages of this exciting adventure she seems quite content with the role of mistress. She gladly settles for whatever he is willing to offer. She is delighted when he takes her out to dinner, or asks her along on a business trip. She never complains and always looks her best. Gradually, the pressure builds up. It begins with the occasional 'wouldn't it be nice if ...'. Then there are hints that other men are interested in this adorable asset. She is happy to be with him, but a girl has to consider her future. What future does she have with someone else's husband?

He wavers. He asks himself if he can live without her. She's such *fun*. But he's not yet ready to commit himself. All kinds of questions demand an answer. What would his children say if he divorced their mother? How much would it cost him? He makes vague promises, hoping that it will enable him to postpone the decision. Eventually, though, the day comes when he has to make up his mind.

Samuel Johnson famously said that a second marriage is a triumph of hope over experience. It may work out, but many rich people go through the process more than once. Sooner or later the new wife is also deemed to be unsatisfactory. The husband may take a mistress, who then goes through the same routine. But there are pitfalls. The discarded partner may threaten to reveal what she knows about his financial manipulations, which can get him into serious trouble, or insist on keeping the shares in his business which he transferred to her because it seemed a smart way to reduce his tax burden.

Divorce is certainly expensive. Ronald Perelman, one of the richest men in America, had to pay $8 million to his first wife, $80 million to his second, and $30 million to the third. He recently divorced his fourth, the actress Ellen Barkin, and said he would give her $20 million. In Britain, the House of Lords issued a ground-breaking rule in 2000 that there should be no automatic bias in favour of the main earner. Sir Martin Sorrell, the advertising mogul, found that parting from his wife after 33 years of marriage cost him a whopping £38 million. She told the court that he 'marginalised' and 'dehumanised' her, 'discarded' her from his affections, and took a mistress.

Not surprisingly, many rich men nowadays ask a potential new partner to sign a pre-nuptial agreement. This first came to prominence in California, where much-married film stars sought to protect themselves against the very real possibility that, in the event of a divorce, they would lose half of their assets. In England, where lifetime maintenance payments are routinely ordered by the courts, they are not viewed as legally binding but they help to show that the new wife accepted the need for limits. In America, they have become commonplace among the nouveau riche.

Donald Trump, the flamboyant property developer, insisted on a pre-nup when he got married for the second time. His first wife, Ivana, had taken him to the cleaners when he dumped her in 1991. He had to give her $10 million in cash, their estate in Greenwich, $650,000 dollars in annual alimony and child support, and a $4-million housing allowance. His new wife, Marla, strongly objected to the idea of a pre-nuptial contract and said so when she and Donald were interviewed on ABC television a few months after marriage. Trump's response was that he, too, hated the idea because it basically says that 'if and when you get divorced, this is what you're going to get'. But, he added, 'I think it's a modern-day necessity'. In the end, he told the interviewer, they had negotiated a deal – she would get a million dollars. 'I built this empire and I did it by myself', he said. 'Nobody did it for me – not Ivana, not Marla, nobody. And I think that because somebody marries someone who has built something huge doesn't necessarily mean that just because they get a divorce they should end up, you know, like the Queen of Sheba.' He and Marla had a daughter (Trump already had three children by Ivana), but he left soon afterwards because, he said, he was bored. She went off to California with her million and more than $8,000 in monthly child support. His new 'girlfriend' was a stunning 25-year-old model, Melania Knauss, and they were married in 2005. 'He's a great man', she told the media. Many other women think he's the worst type of male chauvinist.

You may find it odd that people like him keep trooping down the aisle. There are, after all, plenty of young women who are quite willing to share the life (and lifestyle) of a rich and powerful man without demanding a formal commitment. If he is single, he can play around as much as he likes.

A common reason for serial marriages is that, each time, the man is convinced that he has found someone special and can't bear the thought of losing her. He may change his mind later, but meanwhile he wants to make sure that she doesn't leave him. It would be a personal and public humiliation.

He is often right to be worried. Many women walk away from a relationship because they are tired of waiting for that wedding ring, or because the man has become a bore, or because they have met someone who is better-looking and just as rich. A growing number are wealthy in their own right. They may have inherited money, or started a successful business, or collected a large divorce settlement. They don't want to have children and, like wealthy men, can afford to experiment.

THE FORTUNE HUNTERS

There is obviously some truth in the old saying that the quickest way to a fortune is to marry one. This is certainly the view taken by many people.

Old Money families used to regard fortune-hunting as a duty. Sons and daughters were expected to find a wealthy mate, not merely to ensure their own future comfort but for the sake of the whole tribe. They were provided with an allowance so that they could do it in style. The tradition is still upheld by some families and, in theory, it should be easier to succeed because there are so many more fortunes to hunt. But much has changed.

New Money people have become more adept at protecting their wealth. They have a disconcerting habit of devising financial schemes that keep it beyond the hunter's reach. Many a young man has courted an heiress only to find, after putting in considerable effort, that her money is tied up in a trust fund and can't be touched. Many a woman has made the same discovery about an heir. She would probably have done better to target someone who has created his own fortune and is willing to share it.

The game has some basic rules and you may like to know what they are.

Do your homework

It is essential to investigate the financial status of a prospect before you get too involved. It can be difficult because some people lie. Appearances can be deceptive. A man with a yacht and a Bentley is not necessarily rich; he may have paid for them with borrowed money. A woman with expensive jewellery may *look* wealthy but it may have been given to her by a previous lover. Quite often the intended target turns out to be another fortune hunter.

Go where the rich are

Wealthy people have their own social circle, which you must seek to infiltrate. Make them think that you are one of them. They feel more at ease with their own kind, and once you have been accepted other invitations are sure to follow.

A title still helps, but it has become less important because so many of the nouveau riche, including pop stars, have acquired knighthoods and because titles like Count and Prince no longer have any legal status in European republics.

Cosmopolitan cities like London, Paris and New York are good hunting grounds, but avoid Los Angeles because there is too much competition. In summer, the seriously rich can usually be found in places like Monaco, Cannes, the Hamptons and Newport. In winter, they tend to migrate to Palm Beach, Aspen, Gstaad and St Moritz. Caribbean islands like Barbados and St Barts are also popular, but they attract too many tourists – and as already said, the rich prefer to stay on their yachts.

Never talk about money

It is considered ill-mannered to discuss money on social occasions. It is also bad strategy because it makes people suspicious. Always give the impression that the subject is of little interest, even if your bank manager is getting impatient.

Target the 'elderly'

Older people are usually portrayed as staid and tight with the little money they have. Many fit that description but there are also many who are asset-rich and determined to have a good time.

Research has shown that 70 per cent of wealthy people in Britain are over 55. They include septuagenarian sybarites who still take an active interest in sex and who are prepared to be generous. Some have chosen to remain single after a divorce or the death of their partner; others want to get out of an unsatisfactory marriage. They do not necessarily seek someone who is much younger. Many prefer someone who is nearer to their own age. This is why some of the most success-ful fortune hunters, of both sexes, are themselves over 55.

Here again, though, it is important to do one's homework. Make discreet enquiries; in particular, try to find out if they have transferred most of their assets to their children.

I realise that all this sounds cynical. You may well feel, as I do, that such a blatantly materialistic approach is too sordid to contemplate. Marrying a fortune certainly doesn't guarantee happiness; if money is the only motive, a relation-ship can easily turn sour. I have met many people who regret that they embarked on a loveless marriage – they are rich but unhappy.

CHAPTER 15

THE POWER OF MONEY

For many people, material possessions are not enough. They also want to influence events.

Throughout history, the rich have sought to make and unmake political leaders for a variety of reasons: to secure new territories or conditions favourable to their enterprises, to gain personal advancement, or just for the hell of it. The rules of the game have changed a great deal, but the basic aim has remained the same: to make the world the kind of place *they* want to live in.

For centuries, wealthy men would either buy their own armies or finance those of ambitious people who shared, or claimed to share, their ideas of what their particular corner of the world should be like. Some gloried in the display of power; others shrewdly decided that it was just as satisfying, and usually a lot safer, to pull the strings. Monarchs could be extremely capricious when they felt that they were being upstaged.

The wealthy backers of charismatic politicians often get more than they bargained for. Adolf Hitler is a classic example. When this penniless adventurer joined the German Worker's Party (DAP) in 1919, the party's entire resources consisted of small change. His early efforts to raise cash met with little success, but when the Nazis started to make headway at the polls, a number of industrialists donated considerable sums. Hitler cleverly exploited their fears of communism. They didn't think much of this excitable ex-corporal with his funny moustache, but they were impressed by his following and had no doubt that they would be able to control him. It didn't work out like that, as we all know. When Fritz Thyssen, one of the biggest backers, protested against the invasion of Poland, he was expelled from the party and his fortune was confiscated. Thyssen went into exile in France, but the Vichy regime handed him over to the Gestapo and he was sent to a concentration camp.

In Italy, Mussolini took the same route as Hitler – he persuaded the rich that he was the right man to deal with the 'red menace'. In numerous meetings with business leaders, he talked at length about the need to restore discipline in the factories. Years later the Duce adopted his fellow dictator's racist views and forced his early Jewish backers to emigrate.

The United States, which at times has seemed just as obsessed with the communist threat, has had the good fortune (or perhaps it would be fairer to say good sense) to escape the fate of countries like Germany and Italy. But the rich have been just as eager to involve themselves in the political power game, either by supplying campaign funds to candidates representing their interests or by running for office themselves.

Many presidents have come from wealthy backgrounds or have made it to the White House with financial help from relatives and friends. One well-known example is that of John Kennedy, whose mega-rich father spent lavishly to promote his career.

Lyndon Johnson relied heavily on Texas oilmen. His usual method, during his days as Senate Majority Leader, was to call a potential contributor into his office and tell him exactly how much he was to give, and to whom. If there was any hesitation, he would remind him of pending bills affecting his business interests. His wheeling and dealing, and his establishment of a highly profitable broadcasting network, made him multi-millionaire by the time he reached the Oval Office. But his pursuit of money continued unabated.

Richard Nixon, too, milked every business in the country. Many of the activities associated with the Watergate scandal, which eventually led to his resignation, were financed with illegal or misappropriated campaign contributions.

In 2002, both houses of Congress passed a long overdue Bipartisan Campaign Reform Act. The new law most notably bans unlimited donations to national political parties. But there are still many ways of raising large sums of money. George W. Bush collected a record-shattering $200 million when he decided to go for a second term. The rewards included ambassadorships for wealthy individuals.

The power of money is also at work at the regional and local level in the US. Running for governor of a state, or a seat, is expensive, especially for a challenger. It costs so much to get one's message across in the news media. Most of the funds tend to come from special-interest groups who hope for favours from the winner.

Some candidates are so wealthy that they don't need this kind of help. When Michael Bloomberg ran for the office of Mayor of New York, he dipped into the huge fortune made from his own media empire. He spent $30 million on his first campaign and, according to the local press, another $70 million to make sure that he was re-elected.

It's all quite different in Britain. Ken Livingstone, the Mayor of London, is a pauper compared with Bloomberg and there are few rich people in government. Campaign contributions are made to a party, not to individuals (MPs have strict limits on electoral expenses). The civil service is both more determined and in a better position to preserve its independence. Ambassadors are career diplomats. There are lobbyists and pressure groups but they have less clout than in America. Members of parliament must declare any business connections they may have and any benefits they may receive, including hospitality. Ministers are not allowed to keep the lavish gifts they are so often presented with in other parts of the world, such as the Middle East and Latin America, where bribery is common practice. The Prime Minister used to be able to reward generous contributors to party funds with a knighthood or a peerage, and often did, but had his wings clipped after a storm of protest early in 2006. Several of his peerage nominations were blocked by the House of Lords Appointments Commission and he was forced to accept that there should be a public inquiry. There has also been a lot of fuss in the media about the earnings of his wife, a prominent lawyer, but none of the occupants of 10 Downing Street in modern times have used their office to accumulate a personal fortune.

PUBLISH AND BE PRAISED

No sector, on either side of the Atlantic, has increased its power more rapidly than the media. It can make or break reputations, change policies and ruin political careers.

The press and, more recently, television has always fascinated the rich, not just because the ownership of media offers another opportunity to make money but also because it provides so much scope for self-promotion and for shaping public opinion.

My first boss in journalism, Lord Beaverbrook, was quite blunt about his motives. He told a Royal Commission that he ran his newspapers 'purely for the purpose of propaganda'.

Beaverbrook, then plain Max Aitken, came to Britain from Canada in 1910 as a wealthy man intent on making an impact in politics. He entered parliament as MP for Ashton-under-Lyne, and six years later bought the ailing *Daily Express*. He used the paper for various crusades, including a campaign to bring down the Tory Prime Minister Stanley Baldwin, who famously accused press barons like him of wielding 'power without responsibility: the prerogative of the harlot throughout the ages'.

Beaverbrook served in Churchill's cabinet during the Second World War but never held office again. When he made me City editor of one of his papers, the *Evening Standard,* he was well into his seventies but still very much in charge. We often went for long walks in one of London's parks; he would feed the ducks and talk at length about the business affairs of men he liked or hated, and 'suggest' that I might care to look into them. I was left in no doubt about the line he wanted me to take. He was also fond of biblical quotations, which he would work into the conversation whenever he thought they were appropriate. 'Remember', he once told me, 'the bible says that where your treasure is there your heart will also be.' Beaverbrook died at the age of 85. Michael Foot, who had been a close friend, wrote this about him:

> He was a rampant individualist, and he always favoured the rumbustious marauding of the private enterprise system which had enabled him to become a multi-millionaire. He brought with him, too, a detestation for the stuffiness, stupidities, and snobberies of the English Establishment. He was an instinctive radical.

His son Max continued to run the company but eventually sold it to the Trafalgar House conglomerate. The new boss was Victor Matthews, a plain-speaking cockney who had made a fortune in the building trade. He knew nothing about Fleet Street and offered me the job of editorial director. I said that I couldn't accept because I had established my own magazine-publishing company, but agreed to become his personal assistant, and a Board member, on a part-time basis.

Victor was gratified to discover, soon after taking over, that his new status brought him invitations to lunch with the Prime Minister and other leading politicians, who sought his opinion on a wide range of topics, especially the economy. I was with him for three years, and did what I could to help, but he was no Beaverbrook. I left when he insisted that I had to choose between a full-time involvement, as editor of the *Daily Express*, and my company. I told him that I preferred to do my own thing. It was just as well, because not long afterwards Trafalgar decided to get out of the newspaper business. By then, Victor had secured a peerage.

My purpose in telling the Matthews story in this book is to give the reader a first-hand account of the kind of thing that can happen when a rich businessman is seduced by the glamour of the national press. Plenty of others have been similarly tempted.

The Express group now belongs to Richard Desmond, previously a publisher of porno magazines. He has made the papers more lively but they have yet to regain the formidable reputation they once had.

The *Mirror* was, for a time, owned by the late Robert Maxwell. It made him more powerful than he had been as a backbench MP, but his megalomania and greed led to his ignominious downfall. 'Tiny' Rowland, who had extensive business interests in Africa, bought the *Observer* but got tired of subsidising its heavy losses and sold it to the Scott Trust, the owners of the *Guardian*. Sir James Goldsmith, a contro-versial billionaire, launched a news magazine called *Now!* but it was a costly failure. Mohamed Al-Fayed, the Egyptian owner of Harrods, tried to revive *Punch* (which I had edited for most of the 1970s) but misjudged the market and closed it down after spending millions. Conrad Black, a wealthy Canadian, acquired the *Telegraph* papers and became a British citizen so that he could accept a peerage – but got into trouble with shareholders and was sacked by the Board. The titles now belong to the close-lipped Barclay twins, who made most of their fortune in property. An Irish tycoon, Tony O'Reilly, bought Independent News & Media in 1994.

The world's most influential media magnate, Rupert Murdoch, is an American citizen but was born in Australia. He inherited a small evening paper from his father and acquired others with the help of banks; he also launched a new daily, the *Australian*. Few people in Britain had heard of him until he managed to get hold of the *News of the World* in 1968, at the age of 37. The sleepy Carr family, which had been in charge for many years, were trying to fight off a bid from Robert Maxwell ('that ghastly foreigner') and welcomed Rupert as a white knight from a country they still regarded as part of the British Empire. I was at the noisy meeting of shareholders which settled the issue and was appalled by the crass xenophobia.

Murdoch, never a fan of the Establishment, stayed cool and ousted the family after he won. He transformed the paper into a sex-and-crime tabloid and went on to buy the fading *Sun* from the Mirror Group for a trifling sum. His formula – sharply presented news, racy features and buxom girls – was a tremendous success.

He next turned his attention to America, where he bought the *New York Post* and other titles. But he rushed back to the UK when he heard that the *Times* and *Sunday Times* were for sale. The deal gave him control of more than a third of the British national press, but Fleet Street's trade unions were troublesome. For years they had held managements to ransom by threatening to strike whenever attempts were made to introduce new technology and curb over-manning. Murdoch decided on a course of action which other proprietors, afraid of losing readers, had not dared to contemplate. He provoked a strike and then sacked his print workers, announcing that production would be transferred to a new plant at Wapping, in East London, where modern technology would be used whether they liked it or not. During the year that followed there were ugly scenes outside 'Fortress Wapping', as it became known when he surrounded it with barbed wire. The unions eventually gave in. It was a turning point for the newspaper industry and, looking back, he says that he is 'very, very proud of it'.

In 1990, he launched Sky television. It was another bold gamble, and there were many anxious moments, but it has since become the leading commercial broadcaster. His News Corporation also owns the right-wing Fox network in America and 20th Century Fox films. But he has often said (to me and others) that he remains at heart a journalist. His many enemies accuse him of being a bully and he can certainly be ruthless. He is respected, feared, and loathed in equal measure by politicians and rivals. Presidents and prime ministers court him because they know that he calls the shots – editors who defy him don't last long.

Rupert is reckoned to have a personal fortune of more than $6 billion, but money has always been a means to an end. He hopes that one of his children will succeed him, but that will be up to the financial institutions and others who hold the majority of the shares in News Corporation.

Many people believe that newspapers have a bleak future. Murdoch himself says that 'great journalism will always be needed but the product of their work will not always be on paper – it may ultimately be just electronically transmitted'. But, he adds, for many years to come it will be disseminated by both. He maintains that 'the people of Britain are uniquely lucky to have such a great choice of newspapers and news, whereas in America you don't'. I think he is right about that, though I hate what he has done to the *Times*. I am also sure that, despite TV and the internet, the press will continue to have a lot of influence.

CHAPTER 16

FEARS OF THE RICH

Money can buy many things, but immunity from ill-health is not one of them. Cancer and other diseases hit millionaires and paupers alike. The rich are aware of this disconcerting fact of life, and like everyone else they are afraid of it.

Many consider it unfair – they regard themselves as special and find it hard to cope with sudden, unexpected illness. This is particularly true of powerful tycoons. They are so sure of themselves, and so used to controlling every aspect of their life, that they tend to take good health for granted. They work long hours, eat and drink too much, and take little exercise. The possibility that all this may be cut short seldom occurs to them, or if it does they brush it aside. ('I don't have ulcers, I give them', movie mogul Harry Cohn once told an interviewer.) God gave them talents denied to others; surely he isn't going to take it all away, while allowing ignorant peasants to enjoy glowing health right into old age?

He can, and he does. God is not impressed by a man's bank balance. But doctors are, and the rich have at least one consolation: they know that money *can* buy the very best care.

Private medical services are one of the growth industries of the 21st century. This is particularly true of America, but Britain also has a large number of clinics whose cash-conscious owners cater to the rich and their ailments. Harley Street specialists have made fortunes by treating people (including many foreigners, especially Arabs) who not only demand expert skills but also the kind of luxurious surroundings to which they are accustomed. Their frightened clients will gladly pay whatever is asked.

Many left-wing politicians resent the fact that the rich have such privileges, but they are not a burden on the taxpayer and they relieve the pressure on the National Health Service.

The tremendous advances in medicine have been of benefit to everyone. There has been a vast increase in both the range and the effectiveness of drugs; this has been combined with a significant improvement in surgery, helped by an impressive array of new technology. The much-criticised NHS has many good hospitals. Average life expectancy has risen by three decades since Victorian times; more of us are growing older together than ever before. But cancer and heart disease continue to kill many people, often at an early age. My own son had a fatal heart attack when he was only 45. He, too, had always thought that it couldn't possibly happen to him.

One doesn't have to like the rich to understand their fears; we are all human. But it's a great deal easier to sympathise with those who are truly ill than with those who are merely self-indulgent. The idle rich are often dreadful hypochondriacs. They have so much time on their hands that they tend to be obsessively concerned with their health; every minor ailment is seen as a disaster which requires maximum attention.

Psychiatrists flourish because of wealthy patients. The poor tell their troubles to relatives and friends; the rich rush off to the well-padded couches of expensive shrinks. In New York and California it's almost de rigueur to have one's own psychiatrist; it's as much of a status symbol as a Cadillac or a yacht. Some people really need that kind of help, but many more are simply on an ego trip. It must be boring to listen to their rambling dissertations, but it is undeniably lucrative.

We British like to think that we have more sense, but a growing number of showbiz celebrities also boast about their regular sessions with a shrink. Their problems are often self-inflicted. Many are addicted to recreational drugs, alcohol, or sex. They can afford to indulge themselves, and do so, but find it hard to deal with the consequences – or, like the Hollywood lot, want to impress us. They don't seem to realise how foolish they look.

Many of the rich are also into alleged 'youth treatments'. There is nothing new about this. Cleopatra is said to have bathed in asses' milk, but she didn't live long enough to find out if it worked in old age. Others have tried all kinds of disgusting things, from mud baths to injections of monkey glands. In the decade or so after the Second World War, one of the most famous drugs was Gerovital. Developed by a Romanian scientist, Professor Ana Aslan, it was hailed as a highly effective anti-ageing drug. The Greek shipping billion-aire Aristotle Onassis was a customer, and so was German Chancellor Konrad Adenauer. General de Gaulle and Charlie Chaplin were also reputed to be among her customers. When I visited her institute, her assistants told me that Gerovital slowed the *rate* of ageing, but that it couldn't work miracles. 'The main effect', they said, 'is in the brain – it preserves cheerfulness'.

If Cleopatra were still around today she would no doubt resort to methods like botox, hormone replacement and plastic surgery. In our gerontophobic culture, the medical profession sells not only ways of preventing diseases but also the seductive prospect of eternal youth. Magazines and web-sites push facelifts, breast enhancements, hair transplants, liposuction and a cornucopia of creams and lotions.

The original aim of plastic surgery was to deal with wartime injuries. It is still used to repair or reconstruct a part of the body that has been injured or is malformed, but cosmetic operations are much more common. In America, 'having one's face done' is considered only a shade more adventurous than having one's teeth capped. I once called a clinic in Los Angeles for more information and found myself talking to a recording. 'The sands of time affect all of us', it announced. I barely had time to nod before it added: 'This [cosmetic surgery] is one effective way of turning back the clock'. I shouldn't expect to find a new life, or get rich from my new face, nor should I expect to 'look like a movie star', but an operation would 'improve my appearance and boost my self-confidence'.

A surgeon later told me that he was making more than $500,000 a year. Not all his clients were old: some were in their thirties and forties. Women, he said, generally felt under greater pressure to look good and sexy. Many feared that they might lose their husband or partner to a younger rival. Men were more likely to have something done because they wanted to enhance their marketability. Fading celebrities headed the list, but his clients also included business executives who were worried about losing their job or who believed that they stood a better chance of promotion if they disguised signs of ageing.

A facelift is widely regarded as the definitive age-busting procedure. What is often not realised is that there are risks – facial paralysis, infections, embolisms, skin loss and visible scarring. The positive results don't last for more than eight years or so. Some people have had three or four operations. They no longer look real – an object lesson in how something that is supposed to improve one's appearance can easily have the opposite outcome.

Botox injections have also become fashionable on both

sides of the Atlantic. Botox is a muscle-freezer that erases frown lines and crow's feet. The effects last only for a few months, so it's a multiple procedure. Here again, the patient may end looking creepy. Hollywood directors say that many actresses have gone under the knife so often, and have been pumped so full of Botox, that they can't express any emotion with their faces. I have been to parties in Los Angeles where all the women looked like dolls off the assembly line, with identical button noses and fixed smiles. It may be their idea of beauty, but it isn't mine.

Early in 2006, the media got excited about 'the world's first face transplant'. The patient, a young French woman, had suffered terrible injuries at home and said she was grateful for her surgeon's efforts. There was a lot of silly talk about what this 'breakthrough' might lead to – in future, it was said, the rich would be able to buy an entirely new face. One London surgeon told that, yes, 'face donations' had obviously become feasible but that 'public squeamishness' would be an obstacle.

Scientists are experimenting with other techniques. Many predict that genetic engineering will be the next big thing. Mapping the human genome, they say, has paved the way for a 'medical revolution'. Doctors will be able to detect all kinds of flaws in our genetic make-up and correct them. New drugs will be targeted at specific genes. Most diseases will be eliminated.

It sounds great, but medical revolutions don't happen overnight. It also raises moral and ethical issues. Many people think that the experiments are against the will of God. Some are appalled by reports of cloning, as they feel that scientists cannot be trusted to behave responsibly and observe basic moral laws.

Another point is that the new treatments, if and when they are approved by regulators, are bound to be expensive. The rich don't care about the cost, but what about the rest of us? Should they also be available on the NHS? Can the country afford it?

Some scientists are on record as saying that, by the end of the century, mankind may have achieved immortality. That strikes me as fanciful and undesirable, but I am prepared to believe that life spans may be extended to 110 or even 120 years.

Would I want to live to 110? Yes, if I could be sure that I still had all my faculties. Longevity is not enough; what counts is the number of healthy years one has left. I have met many rich people who are confined to a wheelchair or are suffering from Alzheimer's. *My* worry is that the same may happen to me.

THE PERILS OF FAME

Another fear of the rich is that they will become a target for criminals. It is the main reason why many don't want to see their name on any rich list. Gangs have been known to use such lists for burglary, mugging and kidnapping.

Celebrities are especially vulnerable, as they attract a lot of publicity. Some is welcome – indeed, sought – because it helps to advance their careers. They give press interviews, go on television, and make appearances at public events. Most also have websites devoted to them. The downside of all this attention is that bad buys get to know a great deal about their lifestyle. They have their address, clippings from magazines (including photos of their possessions), details about their family, and other useful information.

Wealthy business tycoons tend to be more cautious, but many are also featured in the media – whether they like it or not. Some are so paranoid that they hire public relations people to keep their name *out* of newspapers.

Security is a thriving industry. Homes can be protected by an array of devices – alarms, cameras, pick-resistant locks, high-intensity floodlights, aggressive dogs, guards, a 'safe room' with emergency lights, and so on. The rich have a wider choice than ever before and, as with healthcare, cost is not an issue. But criminals have also become more sophisticated. Many are experts at dealing with security systems, or work with others who know a way around them.

Robberies are often carried out during the day, rather than at night, because they are reckoned to be easier. A common ploy, particularly in the affluent parts of big cities, is to pose as an official who has 'come to check the meter' or as a 'researcher'. Not long ago, the wife of a wealthy London banker opened the door to a man who said he was delivering a package. She was stabbed and the burglar rushed past her; when her husband – who happened to be at home – came to the rescue, he too was attacked and later died from multiple wounds.

The police frequently arrive long after the event. Officers say that burglary is so common that they don't have time to answer every call, but in many cases there is another reason: they are reluctant to confront a thief who may be armed. Their first question, if no one has been seriously hurt, is whether the victim is insured.

In Britain, the possession of firearms will still get you in serious trouble with the law. In contrast, the rich in America are more likely to have guns and they stand a better chance of being acquitted if they use them. The right to shoot intruders has long been accepted by most courts. Some even keep a hand gun in the glove compartment of their car because they feel more vulnerable outside the home.

Many showbiz stars have a bodyguard, but are uneasily aware that nothing guarantees complete protection. There is always a possibility that someone in a crowd of fans will step forward and shoot them. John Lennon was shot outside his own apartment block in New York. Even presidents – the most closely guarded people in the world – are not safe. Ronald Reagan was shot as he left a hotel after making a speech. He survived, but it was a grim reminder that anything can happen.

A wealthy friend of mine was held up at gunpoint by a couple of thugs when he drove his new Ferrari in the South of France. He knew that it would be foolish to resist and watched, helplessly, as they raced away in the car. When he went to the police, they said that there was nothing they could do. The Ferrari would already be in Italy (the border was nearby) and would be repainted and given a new number plate. He would never see it again; his best course was to call his insurance company.

Another gambit used by professional gangs is to infiltrate a grand event, like a society ball, to see what jewellery the rich are wearing. The infiltrator then passes the information by mobile on to others – who can then follow the target to their home, and confront them before they get inside or rob them while they are sleeping.

Boat theft has also become big business on the French Riviera. Highly organised mafias from Eastern Europe are becoming ever more daring as they steal luxury yachts to order. Territorial waters end twelve miles out to sea, after which pursuing criminals becomes an international affair. Once out of reach of the marine gendarmerie, the thieves often head for Malta or Tunisia, where they register under a bogus offshore company, repaint their booty, and rename it. Next stop is the Black Sea, where they sell the stolen yachts to a growing clientele of nouveau riche, mainly from Russia and the Ukraine. 'It's a kind of money laundering', says the commander of the gendarmerie. The boats are also used for trafficking drugs and weapons.

THE SNATCH RACKET

One of the greatest fears of the rich is that they, or someone close to them, may be kidnapped for ransom. Kidnapping is as old as history, though the word itself goes back only to the 17th century – it was first used to describe 'the trade of decoying and spiriting away young children and shipping them to foreign plantations'. Julius Caesar was abducted by pirates in 78 BC; they collected a ransom, but after he was set free he pursued them and saw to it that they were executed. Richard the Lionheart was kidnapped on his way home from the Crusades in 1192 and held captive for more than a year. And in medieval England, the abduction of wealthy heiresses was so commonplace that the government eventually made it a hanging offence.

In America, the early 1930s saw what newspapers described as an epidemic of the crime – the 'snatch racket'. The most famous case was the kidnapping of the Lindbergh baby, which led to such a public furore that it played a key role in the creation of the FBI. The famous aviator lived with his family in a remote New Jersey farmhouse four miles from the nearest road. Charles Junior was put to bed at the usual time by his nurse. When later that evening she went to check that he was asleep, the cot was empty. There was a ransom note on the windowsill. When the news was made public, it caused a sensation. Lindbergh was a national hero: how could anyone do this to him? More than 100,000 people offered their help – including Al Capone, who was serving a long jail sentence but confidently asserted that, if released, he would get the baby back. Ships and planes were brought in to help with the search. It was all in vain: 72 days after the kidnapping, the body of Charles Jr. was found in a small hollow about a mile from the Lindbergh home.

In 1932, a Federal Kidnapping Bill was passed and a young

man, J. Edgar Hoover, was put in charge of the new law enforcement agency. Hoover declared that he knew of 'no more heinous crime than kidnapping' and his agents went to work. A 35-year-old German carpenter, Bruno Hauptmann, was arrested and hauled before a court: found guilty, he went to the electric chair. By 1939, the epidemic was over.

There have been many other cases on both sides of the Atlantic in recent decades. Two that particularly caught the public eye in the 1970s were the kidnapping of Patty Hearst in California and of Paul Getty III in Rome.

Patty, the attractive 19-year-old daughter of the super-rich newspaper proprietor, William Randolph Hearst, was snatched by an outfit calling itself the Symbionese Liberation Army. She would be released, they said, in exchange for a food distribution programme to the poor of San Francisco. Her father did his best to oblige. He offered to set up a $4 million trust fund at the Wells Fargo Bank and signed a legally binding agreement to release $2 million worth of food if Patty were set free within a month, and a further $2 million nine months later. But then he received an astonishing message, on tape. In it, she accused her parents of 'playing games' and said that she had been given a choice of 1), being released in a safe area or 2), joining the forces of the Symbionese Liberation Army 'and fighting for my freedom and the freedom of all oppressed people. I have chosen to stay and fight.' A few weeks later the gang held up the Hibernia Bank in San Francisco, and photographs taken by the bank's camera showed Patty Hearst, wearing a black wig and brandishing a gun. A wanted poster went up for her arrest. She was eventually captured and sent to jail for seven years. President Carter pardoned her after 22 months and she married her bodyguard.

The kidnapping of Paul Getty III also made headlines and raised questions which are still being asked today. How far should the rich go when they are faced with the same situation? What will the gang do if it doesn't get the cash?

In July 1973, a few days after the teenager had apparently gone missing in Rome, a letter arrived by special delivery at the flat he shared with his German girlfriend, Martine. It was addressed to his mother, Gail, and was in Paul's handwriting.

Dear Mummy,

Since Monday, I have fallen into the hands of kidnappers. Don't let me be killed. Arrange things so that the police don't intervene. You must absolutely not take this thing as a joke.

Try and get into contact with the kidnappers in the manner and the way they tell you to.

Don't let the police know about the negotiations if you don't want me to be killed.

I want to live and to be free again. Arrange things so that the police don't know that I have written from this address. Don't publicise my kidnapping.

This is all you have to know. If you delay, it is very dangerous for me. I love you.

Paul

Martine could not find his mother and decided that, despite Paul's instructions, she had better go to the police. They were sceptical. True, there had been a number of kidnappings in recent months and, as the grandson and namesake of 'the richest man in the world', he was an obvious target. But they suspected that this one might well have been arranged by Paul himself.

He was already well known to them. A rootless and trouble-some young man, he had often been found drunk in dubious nightclubs, and there was evidence that he had been socialis-ing with criminals. The press called him the 'golden hippie' but the police knew that Paul was penniless: he and an Italian friend earned what they could by painting and selling their work to tourists.

Their suspicion grew when Martine revealed that he had talked about arranging his own kidnapping 'to raise money'. But when Paul's mother heard that he was missing, and read the letter, she was convinced that her son was in danger. She immediately sought help from her ex-husband (she and Paul's father had been divorced in 1965) and from the boy's grandfather. The old man, reputed to be worth billions, refused to have anything to do with the affair. He issued a brief statement in answer to all press inquiries: 'Although I see my grandson infrequently, and I am not particularly close to him, I love him nonetheless. However, I don't believe in paying kidnappers. I have fourteen other grandchildren and if I pay one penny now, then I will have fourteen kidnapped grandchildren.'

Getty had been charmed by the boy when he was very young but he thoroughly disapproved of what the 'little rascal' had become. Paul III had antagonised him not only by his behaviour but also by his open expressions of contempt for all that the rich stood for. 'I am a refugee from a Rolls Royce', he had written. 'I am an escapee from the credit card. I can eat one meal a day. And life is a banquet. The rich are the poor people of this earth. They are a suffering minority whose malnutrition is of the spirit. Pity the rich. In terms of living they are beggars.'

Like the police, the older Getty had doubts whether the kidnapping was genuine. But his view that paying a ransom would only encourage more kidnapping was sincerely held.

His refusal was widely publicised and seen as yet another example of the billionaire's legendary meanness.

On 10 November, an express package posted twenty days before in Naples arrived at the Rome office of *Il Messaggero*. Inside it, sealed in a plastic bag, was a human ear with a tuft of blood-encrusted reddish hair and a written note: 'We are the kidnappers of Paul Getty. We keep our promises and send the ear. Now find out if it belongs to Paul. Unless you pay the ransom within ten days, we shall send you the other ear. And then other pieces of his anatomy.'

The newspaper contacted Paul's mother, who immediately identified the ear as his. A forensic expert also confirmed that it had been cut from a living human being and that 'comparisons indicate it belonged to Paul Getty'.

The old man at last recognised that something had to be done. As he subsequently recalled in his autobiography: 'with that [the amputation] it became apparent that there was no hope of outwaiting – or bluffing – the kidnappers. Criminals who would savagely mutilate a victim would not hesitate to kill him.' Publicly, though, he continued to insist that he would not pay any ransom. 'My position is still the same', he said. 'I must consider the safety and welfare of all my grandchildren and the rest of the family. What has happened to my grandson Paul is heartbreaking and I pray that he will be safely returned. But I know that for me to become involved in any ransom could make things worse. It is a lonely decision, but I know it is the right one.' Privately, he told his son, Paul's father, that the ransom should be paid by him because there was no knowing what the kidnappers would demand if they felt that he was ready to give in. It was decided that they should offer a ransom of a million dollars. As Paul II did not have that kind of money, his father agreed to lend him $850,000 at 4 per cent interest, on the understanding that it would be repaid in full. A formal agreement was drawn up.

On 17 November, lawyers acting for Paul Getty II issued a statement in London: 'Mr Getty has offered to pay a ransom to the kidnappers. The amount is the maximum that the father has been able to raise for the return of his boy.' The mother wrote an open letter to the press, pleading with the kidnappers to accept the ransom and release her son:

> We have talked at length, you and I. Always I have felt that you were surprised that the grandfather and father have not been moved by the future of young Paul. You have not believed me. Yet this is the truth. I have interceded with the grandfather and the father. The grandfather has remained firm. But the father has agreed to pay a ransom of one million dollars – more than that he cannot give you. I beg of you: accept the money that has been offered to you. In this supreme moment of my life as a mother, decisive only for the life of my son, I feel only pity. Pity for my Paul, so alone, his adorable face mutilated. Pity for you, who do not know what is good in life.

The kidnappers, however, insisted that $1 million was not enough. In the end, the old man relented: out of the $3.2 million demanded, he would contribute $2.2 million and lend the rest to his son. The money was put into an Italian bank and then withdrawn in small notes, all of which were recorded on microfilm. A Getty associate took the cash to the destination nominated by the kidnappers, on the highway to Calabria. Paul was driven from the hideout to the same highway, blindfolded, and set free. When the local police found him, the seventeen-year-old boy told his rescuers: 'I am Paul Getty. Give me a cigarette. Look, they cut off my ear.'

In London, his father made a brief statement to the press. 'I intend', he said, 'to devote the rest of my energies to teaching the Italians the meaning of the word vendetta. I suggest those associated with the kidnapping would be well advised to sleep always with one eye open.' A spokesman for the senior Getty said it was his 81st birthday and the boy's release was 'the finest present he could have'.

The police eventually tracked down the kidnappers, who turned out to be members of a Mafia-style gang. Paul identified one of the ring-leaders at their trial, and some of them were given jail sentences. Only $17,000 was ever recovered.

You may well feel that a billionaire should have behaved differently. The money was small change to Getty. If he truly loved his grandson, as he claimed, he surely should have acted at once. The decision to make his son repay the loan was certainly bizarre. But many rich people agree with his basic point: give in and there is no telling what it will lead to.

This is also the view of governments who are faced with demands from terrorists. They always insist that they will not negotiate. When an Italian prime minister, Aldo Moro, was kidnapped by a ruthless group calling itself the Red Brigades, his colleagues were adamant that there would be no deal. He wrote letters to them that, day by day, became more accusatory and forlorn. They didn't budge and he was eventually found dead in the boot of a car.

It is hard to imagine that anyone could kidnap a British minister, or the President of the United States, but members of their family are less closely guarded.

I have some personal experience of what it feels like when one is told that there may be a risk. When I was Chairman of the British Tourist Authority, I learned that my name had been found on an IRA hit list. My driver had to take a course in evasive techniques and, for a time, there was an unmarked police car outside my house every day. I knew that, if the IRA really wanted to get me, they were more than likely to succeed. Fortunately it turned out to be a false alarm.

The rich and famous tend to be especially vulnerable when they travel, which is why many use an assumed name. Mr Smith is safer than Mr Rockefeller. Hotel security generally leaves much to be desired and aides are seldom trained to deal with kidnappers.

There are many examples of angry clashes between the families of kidnap victims and the authorities. In Ireland, the 34-year-old heir to a chain-store fortune was dragged out of his car by four masked gunmen. The gang demanded a million dollars, and his wife decided at once that she would pay the ransom. 'I will do whatever the kidnappers want', she said. 'My husband's release is my only priority; I don't care what the authorities' view of the situation is.' But the police were equally determined to stop her, chiefly because they thought that the money could be used to finance terrorist activities. They foiled three attempts to hand it over. The case had a happy ending: the victim was set free after six days. But you can imagine how she would have felt if the gang had carried out its threat to shoot him.

In Italy, there was an outcry when a magistrate announced that henceforth he would block all the assets belonging to the family of someone who had been kidnapped. For a while the move seemed to be quite effective, but then it was found that people had simply stopped going to the police. When the authorities did get to hear of cases they found the families totally uncooperative. Ransom money continued to be paid; they simply borrowed it from wealthy friends. The magistrate had to abandon his hard line.

The police have become better at handling this kind of crime and they have an impressive array of modern technology at their disposal. But things can and do go wrong, and it isn't surprising that anxious families should sometimes see the authorities as an enemy.

In recent years, some gangs have come up with another

ploy: dognapping. Animal rescue experts say that in Britain an average of 950 dogs are abducted every week – nearly 50,000 a year. They warn that the problem will only escalate, as lack of police interest makes dognapping almost risk-free.

The types most often stolen are pedigree breeds with rich owners. Small dogs are especially vulnerable because they are easy to catch and to hide. The owner then gets a call from someone who demands a ransom. Most people pay up because they love their pets and consider them to be part of the family.

Even when the police manage to make an arrest, the courts will want convincing proof of guilt. The dog cannot testify; the thieves also know that courts take a relatively lenient view of this kind of crime. Kidnappers are severely punished; dognappers seldom are.

A friend of mine has hired a retired police officer as a bodyguard for Pumpkin, his Yorkshire terrier. It may sound absurd – dogs are supposed to protect humans, not the other way round – but he reckons that it would cost him a lot more if he had to meet the demands of the 'bastards who think that dognapping is an easy way to make money'.

CHAPTER 17

LAST ACTS

One of the inescapable facts of life which greatly irritates many of the rich is that they can't take their wealth with them when the time comes to leave this world. It strikes them as quite unreasonable that they will have to start all over again, in God knows what circumstances.

The pharaohs, of course, thought that they *could* take it with them, and we are all richer as a result: the contents of just one tomb, that of Tutankhamen, are a magnificent reminder of an ancient civilisation. But the rich discarded that simple belief a long time ago. They have, instead, sought to ensure that they will not be forgotten by making a large donation to a museum, art gallery, concert hall or library. All they ask is that, in return, their name should be emblazoned above the portal.

J. Paul Getty spent a fortune on the creation of a museum in California, which he did not live to see, but which certainly guarantees that millions of us will remember him for many years to come. Others have established foundations devoted to what they considered to be worthy causes. Cecil Rhodes, a British financier who was a great believer in the Empire and who arranged to have a country named after him (Rhodesia, now Zimbabwe), created the prestigious Rhodes scholarships at Oxford University. Alfred Nobel, a Swedish engineer who invented dynamite, left most of his millions in trust to establish five prizes for outstanding work in peace, physics, chemistry, psychology or medicine, and literature.

But some of the rich refuse even to consider the possibility of death. They not only hang on to every penny but stubbornly refuse to make a will. Take the case of Pablo Picasso, who died intestate leaving an estimated $9 million in bank accounts, investments and real estate, plus an enormous treasure of his own works. He must have known what a scramble there would be among his legal heirs and claimants, but he clearly didn't care. Like others before him and since, he apparently feared that once he acknowledged that he was mortal the Grim Reaper would come to get him.

The famously eccentric American billionaire, Howard Hughes, also died intestate. As he left no direct heirs, a bizarre legal battle went on for years. Crooks, forgers, mystics and crackpots all got into the act. The judge who presided over the incredibly complex litigation said he had 'never come across anything like this'. Forty forged wills emerged, including the so-called 'Mormon will', allegedly pushed under the door of the headquarters of the Mormon Church in Salt Lake City, which named garage attendant Melvin Dunmar as a beneficiary. Dunmar told the court that a dishevelled Howard Hughes walked out of the desert and borrowed 25 cents from him. The judge threw out his claim. Many women claimed that Hughes had married them. Actress Terry Moore said that the tycoon married her aboard a yacht in international waters off California, and that they had a child who died in 1952. This claim was also dismissed after the court learned that she was married to someone else at the time. Dozens of frauds insisted that Hughes was their father, and the poor judge was besieged by nutters. 'Three men', he later recalled, 'came through my door declaring: "I'm Howard Hughes – can I have a cheque?" Two of them were black.'

There is no telling what goes through a person's mind when he or she comes to write a last will and testament. The norm is to express love and gratitude for those left behind by making various bequests. But sometimes due to senility, vindictiveness, momentary anger, helplessness, or even a sense of humour, the bequests take unforeseen and unlikely turns. Shakespeare left Anne Hathaway nothing but his 'second-best bed'. And I have always liked the eloquent bitchiness of the rich Englishman who wrote in his will:

> Seeing that I have had the misfortune to be married to the aforesaid Elisabeth, who, ever since our union, has tormented me in every possible way; that was not content with making game of all my remonstrances, she has done all she could to render my life miserable; that Heaven seems to have sent her into the world solely to drive me out of it; that the strength of Samson, the genius of Homer, the prudence of Augustus, the skill of Pyrrhus, the patience of Job, the philosophy of Socrates, the subtlety of Hannibal, the vigilance of Hermogenes, would not suffice to subdue the perversity of her character; that no power on earth can change, seeing that we have lived apart during the past eight years, and that the only result has been the ruin of my son, whom she has corrupted and estranged from me; weighing maturely and seriously all these considerations, I have bequeathed, and I bequeath, to my said wife Elisabeth the sum of one shilling.

Similar thoughts inspired the wealthy American banker who wrote:

To my wife I leave her lover and the knowledge that I wasn't the fool she thought I was. To my son I leave the pleasure of earning a living. For twenty-five years he thought the pleasure was mine, but he was mistaken. To my valet I leave the clothes he has been stealing from me regularly for ten years, also the fur coat he wore last winter while I was in Palm Beach. To my chauffeur I leave my cars. He has almost ruined them and I want him to have the satisfaction of finishing the job.

Both at least had a sense of humour. It is, alas, comparatively rare: far more wills are grim denunciations of relatives who have failed to live up to expectations. Some are written a few hours before death, in a sad attempt to get revenge from the grave. In Germany, some years ago, relatives were asked to hold a wake in an upper floor of the dead man's house. When they were all gathered around the coffin, the floor collapsed and most of the mourners were killed. It was later discovered that he had sawed through the supporting beams.

Some people express their hate not just for one person but for a whole race. There was, for example, the Englishman who died in what he considered was an exile in Tipperary and left a handsome sum:

> ... to be spent on the purchase of a certain quantity of the liquor vulgarly called whisky. It shall be publicly given out that a certain number of persons, Irish only, not to exceed twenty, who may choose to assemble in the cemetery in which I shall be interred, on the anniversary of my death, shall have the same distributed to them. Further, it is my desire that each shall receive it by half-a-pint at a time till the whole is consumed, each being likewise provided with a stout oaken stick

and a knife, and that they shall drink it on the spot. Knowing what I know of the Irish character, my conviction is that, with these materials given, they will not fail to destroy each other, and when in the course of time the race comes to be exterminated, this neighbourhood, at least, may perhaps be colonised by civilised and respectable Englishmen.

Most of us believe that we have the right to decide what should happen to our money when we have gone, but if large amounts are involved our wishes might be challenged in the courts. Many rich people try to prevent this. John Lennon, who was said to be worth $150 million when he was assassinated in New York, included a provision in his will that if any named beneficiary 'objects or takes court action in any way, then I direct that such legatee or beneficiary shall receive nothing whatsoever'. Threats like this don't always work, because the claimants know that judges have the final say.

Wills are a major source of family strife. The rich are often at their worst when they fight over the fortunes left behind by parents and other kin. In the course of these disputes a lot of dirty family linen tends to get washed in public, and in many cases the principal victim of abuse is the benefactor. A notorious example is the court action brought by relatives of Cornelius Vanderbilt who felt that they had been unjustly treated. They argued that his will should be set aside because he was insane at the time he made it. The basis for their claim was that he believed in messages from the dead and in supernatural visions. The judged ruled that such belief in spiritualism did not itself establish proof of insanity.

The courts also showed little sympathy for the daughter of a rich, woman-hating American who stipulated that his estate should go into a trust for 75 years, where it would accumulate interest. The millions should then be used for the building of a library that would bear his name. The words 'No Women Admitted' had to be cut in stone over the main entrance; only books by men would be allowed; magazines would be censored to omit articles by women. Nothing in the design, decoration or appointments should suggest feminine influence. The daughter, who had been left just $5, failed to win her case. This was before women's lib changed attitudes: today she would probably get a different verdict.

Many rich people leave substantial sums, and even property, to their pets. Jonathan Jackson of Columbus, Ohio stipulated that a cats' home should be built, and gave instructions on how it should be laid out: there were to be dormitories, a refectory, grounds for exercise, gently sloping roofs for climbing, rat-holes for sport, an auditorium where the cats were to meet every day and listen to an accordion for an hour (the instrument was the nearest approximation he could think of to a cat's voice), and an infirmary. A surgeon and a nurse were to be employed to look after the cats.

Allen Foster of Little Rock, Arkansas was really hard up for companionship. For more than two years before his death, his only friend was a large Rhode Island hen. Foster willed that after he was gone the hen should be maintained in the manner to which she had become accustomed. Local legend has it that the hen was so arrogant after she became an heiress that she was ostracised by all the others and died, lonely, at an advanced age.

Similar provisions are often made for dogs and even parrots and canaries. The bequests may be challenged on the grounds that the owner was of 'unsound mind' – the euphemism used by lawyers for 'mad'. Judges, who probably have pets of their own, expect convincing evidence, but the usual outcome is a compromise: the relatives promise to take good care of Kitten or Fido if they get the assets. It is a promise that shouldn't be hard to keep. Pets have a comparatively short lifespan. Many are elderly when their owners die. Pets cannot have bank accounts, credit cards or property, so there is a limit to how much of a legacy they can gallop through.

In America, some people have established trust funds for their furry friends. They provide a regular flow of money for the care of one or more animals in the event of the owner's disability of death. But lawyers warn that if the fund is excessively large it is bound to be contested. They also point out that trustees have been known to cheat: when the dog died it was replaced by a lookalike so that they could continue to receive cash. The best way to prevent fraud, they say, is to get a DNA sample of the pet.

Families can be extraordinarily callous. It is not unusual for sons and daughters to squabble quite openly about the estate of an ageing relative while he or she is still alive. Everyone not only feels entitled to a major share but also makes plans for spending it. Anyone who tries to be nice to him, or her, is regarded as a threat. I have actually heard people arguing in front of prospective benefactors, as if their views and feelings were unimportant.

There are several ways of dealing with such insensitivity. The first is to unsettle everyone by living to 90 and developing a sudden enthusiasm for round-the-world trips or a new yacht. It is worth hanging on just to see their faces when you announce yet another expensive project. The second is to get married again and do your best to produce an unexpected heir. The third is to keep threatening to do both these things – and, for good measure, to hint at other madcap schemes you might just get around to. It's an interesting way of passing the time, and an almost foolproof way of getting attention.

Some of the rich amuse themselves, in their later years, by changing their will at frequent intervals. They let it be known that they make a habit of doing so, because it gives them a satisfying sense of power.

One Texas multi-millionaire rewrote his will when he discovered that his son had fired the top executives of the family firm, and replaced them with employees of his own choice, while the old man was in hospital suffering from a bad gallbladder. The son had assumed that because of his age and serious illness, his father was about to die. But he rose from his sickbed and went home. When he learned what had happened, he cut off the son with one dollar and left the bulk of his $400-million estate to charity.

In another case, the wealthy owner of a pharmaceutical company left his entire fortune – more than $500 million – to his Polish-born third wife, Barbara, who had once been employed as a cook/chambermaid by his second wife. The six children held a council of war and decided to go to court. They charged that their father, who had made more than 30 wills over the years, was senile when he executed the final document. They also brought charges of undue influence, fraud and duress against their stepmother and her lawyer. The battle that followed was one of the most sensational, and expensive, in American legal history. More than 200 lawyers had a hand in it, and their fees were estimated at a staggering $24 million. The trial lasted for seventeen weeks, and there were accusations of bribery and intimidation of witnesses, death threats against the judge, and even a riot in court.

The key issue was the personality and behaviour of the 'Polish woman', who had married the multi-millionaire when she was 34 and he was 76. Witnesses for the children painted a picture of a senile old man whose life with their stepmother had been a nightmare of isolation, coercion, physical violence and mental torture. Their lawyers alleged that, against his will or without his realisation, he had placed the estate under her control a few weeks short of his 88th birthday.

Her lawyers told a different story. According to them, he

had left all that money to Barbara because he was madly in love with her, because he wanted to avoid paying unnecessary taxes, and because he had become increasingly disillusioned with the profligate and wasted lives of his children. They had brought suit through 'disappointed greed and envy'. The lawyers produced 41 witnesses who testified that the old boy was competent, kind, sentient to the end, aware of current events, and grateful for the love of his wife, who had cared for him with the utmost devotion.

The court had to decide which version was the truth. It turned out to be harder than either of the parties had envisaged. In the process, reputations (including that of the benefactor) were attacked with a viciousness that surprised even the sensation-hungry press. In the end, the two sides – weary of four months of courtroom argument – did what they surely ought to have done in the first place: they reached a settlement.

The question of 'undue influence' is often the most difficult to resolve. Many outsiders have walked into a fortune by showing kindness to a rich but lonely stranger. When Alice B. Atwood, granddaughter of the founder of the King Ranch in Texas, died at the age of 85, a Chicago policeman who had befriended her was the sole beneficiary. Her relatives went to court but he walked away with millions. The same happened in Britain some years ago, though the amount involved – £200,000 – was more modest. An 80-year-old widow left it to a policeman who, as the judge put it, 'came roaring up the drive on his motorcycle and into her life'. The relatives said that he had 'made up to her' because he knew she was rich, but the judge ruled against them. It might have been a hopeless love, he said, but she was of sound mind when it happened.

Doctors sometimes benefit from wills and may find it harder to prove that they have not resorted to 'undue influence'. This also goes for lawyers who have helped to produce the document.

Because so many rich people die without leaving any known heirs, a new profession has emerged: the bounty hunter. He is usually a trained genealogist, and he specialises in tracking down people who may have a right to unclaimed fortunes. The process can take years, and he collects a handsome reward – usually 35 to 50 per cent of their inheritance.

Wills are often used to pass on some final words of well-intentioned advice. A classic example is the one dictated two months before his death by Jack Kelly, the father of the late Princess Grace of Monaco.

'This', he said, 'is my Last Will and Testament and I believe I am of sound mind. Some lawyers will question this when they read my will; however, I have my opinion of some of them, so we are even.' He went on to list various bequests to his wife, children and servants. 'In the case of my daughters' husbands', he said:

> they do not share and if any of my daughters die, her share goes to her children, or if there are no children, then that share goes back into my own children's funds. I don't want to give the impression that I am against sons-in-law – if they are the right type, they will provide for themselves and their families and what I am able to give my daughters will help to pay the dress shop bills, which, if they continue as they started out, under the able tutelage of their mother, will be quite considerable.
>
> I can think of nothing more ghastly than the heirs sitting around listening to some representative reading a will. They always remind me of buzzards awaiting the last breath of the stricken. Therefore I will spare you that ordeal and let you read the will before I go to my reward – whatever it will be. I do hope that it will never

be necessary to go into Court over spoils, for to me the all-time low in family affairs is a court fight, in which I have seen some families engage. If you cannot agree, I direct that the executor or trustees, as the case may be, shall decide all questions of administration or execution, as the executor and trustees will be of my choosing or yours.

Then came some other advice. 'US government bonds', he said, 'were the best investment even if the return was small. As the years gather you will meet some pretty good salesmen who will try to sell you everything from stock in a copper or gold mine to some patent that they will tell you will bring in millions, but remember that for every dollar made that way millions have been lost. I have been taken by this same gentry but that was perhaps because I had to learn from experience – when my father died, my hopes were high, but the exchequer low, and the stock market was on the other side of the railroad tracks, as far I was concerned.'

'To Kell [his son, John Brendan Kelly] I want to say that if there is anything to this Mendelian theory, you will probably like to bet on a horse or indulge in other forms of gambling – so if you do, never bet what you cannot afford to lose and if you are a loser, don't plunge in to try to recoup. That is wherein the danger lies. There will be another deal, my son, and after that, another one. Just be moderate in all things and don't deal in excess. (The girls can also take that advice.) I am not going to regulate your lives, as nothing is quite as boring as too many "don'ts". I am merely setting down the benefit of my experience, which most people will admit was rather broad, since it runs from Port Said to Hawaii, Miami Beach to South America.'

He added: 'As for me, just shed a respectful tear if you think I merit it, but I am sure you are intelligent enough not to weep all over the place. I have watched a few emotional acts at graves, such as trying to jump into it, fainting etc., but the thoroughbreds grieve in heart.'

'I have ranged far and wide, have really run the gamut of life. I have known great sorrow and great joy. I had more than my share of success. Up to this writing my wife and children have not given me any heartaches, but on the contrary, have given me much happiness and a pardonable pride, and I want them to know I appreciate that. I worked hard in my early life, but I was well paid for that effort. In this document I can only give you things, but if I had the choice to give you worldly goods or character, I would give you character. The reason I say that, is with character you will get the worldly goods because character is loyalty, honesty, ability, sportsmanship and, I hope, a sense of humour.'

'If I don't stop soon, this will be as long as *Gone with the Wind*, so just remember, when I shove off for greener pastures or whatever it is on the other side of the curtain, that I do it unafraid and, if you must know, a little curious.'

FAITH, HOPE AND CHARITY

A will in which all or a major part of the fortune goes to charity is hard to challenge because it seems selfish to do so, and because the courts generally respect the wishes of the benefactor. Like most of us, judges take the view that giving one's millions to some cause is a laudable gesture.

For centuries the rich mainly left their money to the Church, in the hope that it would secure them a place in heaven. This is not as widespread in Christian communities as it used to be, but people of other faiths – notably Muslims – still believe that generosity will be rewarded in the next life.

I mentioned earlier that many of the rich donate sizeable

sums to museums or art galleries because they want to see their names emblazoned above the portal. This also applies to hospitals, colleges and research institutes. In many cases, the donations are made during their lifetime. The fact that they can get tax concessions doesn't make them less valuable.

People who devote their later years to philanthropy are often said to feel guilty about the tactics they used to get rich: their payments are described as conscience money. There is nothing new about this. It was alleged to be the main reason why some of the American robber barons gave away most of their wealth. Andrew Carnegie sought to erase his reputation as a ruthless slave-driving steel magnate by endowing free libraries across the land. (It was Carnegie who famously said that 'he who dies rich, dies disgraced'.) John D. Rockefeller used his vast fortune systematically to identify and attack important public health problems. More recent billionaires like Bill Gates and George Soros have continued the tradition. When Ted Turner, the founder of CNN television, gave a billion dollars to the UN in 1997, he quoted Carnegie and mocked his fellow billionaires: 'What good is wealth sitting in the bank?' The rich lists, he said, were really lists of shame.

Bill Gates is, today, the biggest philanthropist of all. His foundation has a staggering $29 billion in assets and in the seven years since its creation has poured money into efforts to make vaccines for AIDS and malaria, and paid for clinical trials of experimental tuberculosis drugs. Bill's pledge that he and his wife, Melinda, will give away 95 per cent of their wealth has been met, in some quarters, with the old 'conscience money' argument but he sees no reason why he should feel guilty about his success in business. Nor do I. Why is it so hard for cynics to accept that some rich people genuinely want to do good and believe that they can do a better job than politicians?

Americans tend to be more charitable than the British – it's part of their culture. Some wealthy Brits maintain that our government has taken over the roles of the philanthropists in healthcare, education and social services, to which Americans devote much of their giving. They also claim that there is less need to support the arts because so much of the National Lottery money is used for that purpose. It seems a lame excuse, but let's be fair: many rich people make a substantial contribution to charity. Some do so because they want a knighthood, but that is by no means the only motive.

One of the best-known givers is Sir Elton John. He already has his gong, so there clearly are other reasons for his generosity. His AIDS Foundation, which operates on both sides of the Atlantic, has done a lot to help. Sir Elton not only donates a sizeable chunk of his income but also uses his high profile to raise money at various events. Another entertainer who does this on a regular basis is Eric Clapton. His foundation runs a rehabilitation centre in Antigua for people around the world with drug, alcohol, or other compulsive disorders.

Charity auctions have become commonplace. Many are glamorous, star-studded affairs designed to attract the rich. The footballer David Beckham and his wife Victoria invited 500 VIP guests to a Full Length and Fabulous Ball, with sets by Robbie Williams and James Brown, and raised £2 million for children's charities. A wealthy Russian, Evgeny Lebedev, teamed up with *Tatler*'s Geordie Greig, for an auction at Earl Spencer's stately home, Althorp. The guests were treated to beluga caviar and Cristal champagne, live music from the Black Eyed Peas and horse ballet from the Russian cavalry, all to raise funds for Russian children with cancer. The French financier Arki Busson, ex-husband of the model Elle Macpherson, gave a lavish party for 1,000 people and smashed charity auction records, generating more than £18 million for his pet cause, Ark. Henry Wyndham, the Chairman of Sotheby's, organised a Dream Auction for the National Society for the Prevention of Cruelty to Children, with prizes such as a Gulfstream package to St Moritz to do the Cresta Run and a helicopter trip to Paris Couture and dinner with Valentino. It raised more than £5 million.

Not everyone wants these kinds of incentives. Some of the biggest donors prefer to keep a low profile. Families like the Sainsburys and the Westons give many millions to charity without feeling the need to make a public display of their generosity. Some made or inherited their fortune elsewhere but later decided to live in Britain.

The Swedish brothers Hans and Gad Rausing came to London with their families in 1983, mainly to escape from Sweden's punitive tax regime. They had an estimated fortune of £7 billion between them, which came from their co-owner-ship of a packaging company founded by their father in 1950. The enterprise first flourished through the invention of the Tetra Pak, the efficient and hygienic wax container, and under their direction it grew to be the world's largest supplier of cartons and bottles for milk, soups, fruit juices and other liquid products. Today what is now the Tetra Laval Group employs 20,000 people in more than 100 countries.

When Hans reached the age of 70 in 1995, he sold his 50 per cent to Gad for about £4.4 billion. He invested in other products but much of the money went into a range of charit-able trusts, which give away an estimated £40 million a year. His brother later moved to Switzerland, where he died in 2000. Hans made donations to various causes, including a new mathematics centre at Cambridge University and brain tumour research. 'Money above a certain level', he said, 'must be looked upon as a tool to do something and achieve something.'

The Rich

His daughters, Lisbet and Sigrid, have their own charitable foundations. Lisbet, a historian and research fellow of Imperial College, London, is chair of her own Lisbet Rausing Charitable Fund, which has given grants to different charitable groups totalling tens of millions, and has also given £20 million to the Endangered Languages Project. She told the *Independent*: 'Often Americans say "oh, my wealth is a terrible burden". I feel enormously lucky. It brings opportunities and extra responsibilities, but it is not a burden.'

Sigrid studied history at York University and then did a PhD in anthropology at University College, London. Her husband, Eric Abraham, is an Oscar-winning film producer and they have a large house in London and a 40,000-acre estate in the Scottish highlands. But, like her sister, she is a generous philanthropist. Her trust, founded in 1995, gave away £60 million in the first decade of its existence and, she says, will in future distribute £15 million a year. Her causes include human rights, women's rights and environmental groups. She supports refugees from Burma, sex-trafficked women from Albania, Ethiopian women damaged in childbirth, indigenous tribes in Colombia, and slum dwellers in Kenya. She gives money to protect child workers, to educate people about landmines, to limit toxic waste, and to fight discrimination against gays and lesbians.

In 2005, Sigrid made headlines when she bought the literary magazine *Granta* and its publishing arm, Granta Books. 'I intend to ensure that both have the resources to flourish', she said.

As usual, cynics argue that the Rausing sisters *ought* to feel guilty about the wealth they have inherited because they have done nothing to deserve it. Perhaps not, but they have certainly used much of it to help others – often people who have been neglected by governments and exploited by big corporations.

224

Many young inheritors, today, are more idealistic than their forebears. They tend to be better educated and more and more concerned about issues like the environment. One can disagree with their choice of causes, but we should at least acknowledge that they are making a significant contribution.

CHAPTER 18

ROOM AT THE TOP

You may feel by now that being rich is not such a good thing after all. Indeed, you may well have held that view all along: this book may merely have helped to convince you that you were right. But there *are* a great many people who would love to be rich, and who would be disappointed if I did not make some attempt to show how this desirable state can be achieved. We have looked at the careers of a number of fortune-builders, past and present, and they should have provided some clues. But most people want to be given a magic formula – a simple recipe, with no ifs and buts, for making a fortune.

Many authors have tried to oblige them. There have been hundreds of books with titles like *The Success Trip* and *The Success System That Never Fails*. A few have been written by men who have actually made millions, but most of the authors have been academics and others who have merely studied the subject. I hate to be a spoilsport, but if there is one thing I have learned – from personal experience as well as observation – it is that *there is no magic formula.*

Success is the result of many different things, or a combination of all of them: luck, optimism, imagination, focus and the ability to think big.

All successful men and women have their share of sleepless nights. There is a point in every deal when you wonder if you have pulled off a coup or committed yourself to a disaster. The Hollywood producer who has spent $100 million on a movie worries that it may flop at the box office. The impresario who has invested his money in a new play knows that he may lose it all. The entrepreneur who has started his own business may run into all kinds of trouble.

The only safe generalisation, it seems to me, is that one should always beware of generalisations. Horatio Alger, the author of one of the most widely read self-help books of all time, maintained that the key to riches was hard work and more hard work. But there are countless people around the world who have worked like demons all their life without getting anywhere. There are also many people who have made fortunes from financial deals with the minimum of effort. Alger himself died flat broke.

Schoolteachers and parents have a vested interest in persuading the young that academic accomplishments will automatically lead to financial success. It doesn't follow at all. Many academically brilliant young men and women make very little money, however hard they try. Schooling can often breed conformity rather than originality, which is why some of the people I have profiled in the book chose to leave school as soon as they could.

I have interviewed many other drop-outs over the years. Soichiro Honda, the founder of the motor company, told me that he was not impressed by diplomas. 'They don't do the work. I went to a technical high school, but was dismissed. I was twenty-eight when I joined, and I had already held down a job. I attended only the classes I wanted to go to. Other students memorised the lessons, but I compared them with my practical experience. My marks were not as good as those of others, and I didn't take the final examination. The principal called me in and said I had to leave. I told him that I didn't want a diploma. They had less value than a cinema ticket. A ticket a least guaranteed that you would get in. A diploma guaranteed nothing.' Honda, of course, went on to become one of the most successful engineers of his generation.

Ray Kroc, the founder of the ubiquitous McDonald's chain, also left school at an early age. He did various jobs before starting a small Chicago company that distributed Multimixers – machines that could make a number of milkshakes at a time. The business did reasonably well, but it didn't make him rich. One of his customers was a restaurant in California, run by Jack and Dick McDonald. It was using eight of his mixers – more than anyone else. Intrigued, he went to see their operation for himself. The brothers, he found, were doing a roaring trade in hamburgers and milkshakes. When he asked why they didn't open more restaurants, they said that they were quite content to stick to the one they already owned. One told Kroc: 'See that house up there? That's home to me, and I like it there. If we opened a chain, I'd never be home.' They agreed to let him franchise their outlets anywhere in the country for one half of 1 per cent of the gross receipts. He opened his first McDonald's, which he owned himself, in a Chicago suburb the following year and others quickly followed. He decided to buy the brand name outright for $2.7 million. By the mid-1970s, he had franchise holders all over the world and the chain's annual turnover was several billion dollars a year. His personal fortune was estimated at $300 million.

Kroc used to have a plaque in his office which said:

Nothing in the world can take the place of persistence. Talent will not: nothing is more common than unsuccessful men with talent. Genius will not; unrewarded genius is almost a proverb. Education will not; the world is full of educated derelicts. Persistence and determination are omnipotent.

Another remarkable man I met around the same time was Masaru Ibuka, the co-founder of Sony. He began his career as an obscure inventor after graduating in engineering. He failed the entry examination for lifetime employment at Toshiba and decided to start his own small business. He was fortunate enough to find a partner, Akio Morita, who had a flair for finance and marketing. They had met during the Second World War on a Japanese research project and in 1946 set up operations in a small corner room on the third floor of a war-ravaged Tokyo department store building. They had little capital and struggled to produce automatic rice cookers. They also repaired radios and sold short-wave converters to Japanese radio owners hungry for foreign news. The experience taught him that 'it is easier to earn a living by doing something others are not doing'. It remained his guiding principle.

The company was incorporated in 1946. Its prospectus, written by Ibuka, expressed some of his visionary qualities. 'At this time of inception of the New Japan', he wrote, 'we will try to create conditions where persons can come together in a spirit of teamwork, and exercise to their hearts' desire their technological capacity. Such an organisation could bring untold pleasure and untold benefits.' Sony would 'emphasise activities that large enterprises because of their size cannot enter, utilising to the utmost the unique features of our firm, welcoming technical difficulties and focusing on highly sophisticated products of great usefulness to our society'.

Sony's early product was the tape recorder, then still a truly original concept in the Japanese market. But the big break came when Ibuka visited the United States to see if it would sell there, and instead found out about semiconductor technology. He made a down payment of $25,000 to license it from Bell and, on his return, persuaded Morita that there was a bright future for transistor radios. He recognised that the full potential of the transistor – to make a pocket radio – required miniaturisation of all the parts. Most of the component manufacturers thought it was an impossible task but Ibuka persisted and, by the time Sony launched its radio in international markets, the company and its subcontractors had taken the world lead in miniaturisation. As we all know, it went on to pioneer many other leading consumer products.

When I interviewed him in Tokyo, he said that his strength lay in finding and developing new ideas. 'In my field, research and development cannot be left to a department. I take the view that the president, or the chairman, must be directly in charge. He must recognise its importance, and push it in the right direction.'

Sony's philosophy, he added, was to develop a product when there is no market and then to create one. He told me one of his partner's favourite stories. Two shoe salesmen find themselves in a rural, backward part of Africa. The first wires back to his head office: 'There is no prospect of sales. No one wears shoes here.' The other wires: 'No one wears shoes here. We can dominate the market. Send all possible stock.'

Ibuka died some years ago but Sony has continued to be an innovative organisation. His belief that the boss must be the main driving force is shared by Bill Gates, Steve Jobs and many others.

In Britain, one of the more recent success stories is that of Charles Dunstone, the founder of Carphone Warehouse. He started the company in 1989 with £6,000 of his own savings and it is now Europe's largest retailer of mobile phones.

Born into a secure family background, Charles went to boarding school when his parents were posted abroad. He later gained a place at Liverpool University, to read business studies, but called them to say that he didn't intend to go. 'I was bored with unproductive learning', he says. 'I wanted to do things, to make things happen.'

He got a job as a sales executive with a Cambridge computer firm. When the business later changed hands, Charles moved to NEC, the Japanese technology group, where he became a sales manager in the fast-growing area of mobile phones. After three years he realised that there was no reason why he couldn't do for himself what he was doing for NEC. It cost little to enter the market and the time was right. He set up in business from a flat in a Marylebone mansion block and in 1990 opened his first shop with a partner, Guy Johnson. They were soon joined by David Ross, who gave up his career as a chartered accountant at Arthur Andersen.

NEC and others were selling mobiles to large corporate clients. Charles decided focus on people with really small businesses who didn't have a big office structure behind them. Plumbers and builders, for example, would be able to get new work while they were working.

Rapid expansion followed. By 1999, the company had 173 outlets in the UK and another 100 in mainland Europe. It went public in 2000.

Carphone Warehouse is an odd name. There is nothing necessarily wrong with it and, since it has formidable strength as a brand, it would be foolish to drop it. But Carphone Warehouse doesn't sell car phones (although mobiles used to be called that). On the Continent, the company trades as 'Phonehouse', which is more apt.

We can safely assume that virtually everyone who wants and can afford a mobile now has one. Today the market is mostly about replacing and upgrading devices. The speed of technological advance shows no signs of slowing, and customers across Europe are trading in their older models for jazzier new ones, with cameras, music players and full-scale internet access.

The more upgrades there are, the better it is for Charles and his team. They have a lot of regular customers and get recurring revenue from the new contracts they sign up to mobile networks. This churn-driven source of growth may have some years left in it yet, but they have extended their offerings beyond the sale of phones to providing fixed line calls, broadband and international call services. The aim is to become an all-round telecoms services provider.

Now in his early forties, Charles is said to be worth more than £800 million – a valuation based mainly on his share stake. He is inundated with requests from university students writing their dissertations about him; they are often surprised to learn that he has no degree. He tells them that what he has done is all applied common sense. Asked if he plans to take it easy in future, he says that he still loves his work. 'If you cut my arms off it probably says CPW inside like a piece of rock.'

I said earlier that success takes a combination of many things. Let's take a closer look at some of these ingredients.

Luck

We all need some luck, but few things irritate entrepreneurs more than to be told that their success is all due to luck. It implies that they are rich only because they got breaks denied to others. As they see it, opportunities arise all the time. Most people find reasons to ignore or reject them. They tell themselves that the risks are too great, or that 'this is the wrong time to do it', or that 'I'm too busy doing something else'. When others spot a potential opportunity, and make a go of it, we call them lucky when all they have really done is to exploit the opening we chose to miss.

Optimism

Unless you are optimistic about a venture you will, obviously, never launch it. Once it's underway, it may fail. But you can't win if it's never launched at all.

One of the biggest obstacles to success is fear of failure. Many people suffer from anticipatory dread, which has a paralysing effect. Successful entrepreneurs have a total belief in what they are trying to achieve. They don't dwell on setbacks; they learn from them. They will look at things that haven't worked and analyse why they didn't. It is the constant belief that there will always be a way forward that separates the winners from everyone else. With that comes the confidence to change direction when it becomes clear that the path they are pursuing is not going to lead anywhere. They are not afraid to start again. It is the ability to bounce back after a failure that is the hallmark of a good entrepreneur.

People who quit when the going gets tough will never have the pleasure of seeing the venture grow and make millions. The same is true of showbiz and sport. A producer whose movie has flopped will not blame his failure on bad luck; he will seek to persuade investors that the *next* one is going to be a hit. Tennis stars may lose the first set of an important match, and even the second, but they don't despair. They sit there, in the brief interval between games, and you can see the determined look on their faces. They are going to raise their game, try harder, unsettle their opponent with dazzling strokes. If they don't succeed, they tell everyone how much they look forward to the next tournament.

Imagination

As we have seen, another attribute of successful people is imagination. Everything created was first imagined. It may have been a new product or a new way of doing things.

Ideas can come from anywhere. Bill Gates read about a small computer kit in a magazine, *Popular Electronics*, and decided that personal computers had a great future if someone could come up with the right software. Alan Sainsbury 'discovered' the supermarket concept in America and imported it to Britain. Helena Rubinstein got into the cosmetics business because, on a visit to Australia, she was shocked by the dry, rough skins of Australian women and reckoned – correctly – that they would welcome the creams that her mother made in Poland. Anita Roddick had the idea for her business, the Body Shop, during a year-long trip around the world at the age of 25. She learned how women from other cultures cleaned and cared for their skin and hair, and thought that products made from their natural recipes would also have a market at home.

Today many entrepreneurs get ideas from the internet. What they all have in common is a vision of how they can be turned into a commercial success. Their inspirational inventiveness often totally defies convention.

Focus

Although they are always ready to explore new opportunities, most are also good at setting personal and professional goals. They recognise that enthusiasm has to be focused: motivation comes from having a clearly defined target to which you can direct your flow of energy.

Stephen Leacock, the famous Canadian economist, once said about a friend that 'he jumped upon his horse and rode madly off in all directions'. Some entrepreneurs are like that, but the majority are specific about what they are after. It is seldom anything as vague as: 'I'm going to start a business and make lots of money.' They have a strategic plan and strong powers of concentration. Each project is tackled with single-minded determination.

Many of us tend to confuse activity with accomplishment. We rush from one meeting to another, fuss over details, and allow ourselves to get sidetracked by things that happen outside work. Successful entrepreneurs concentrate on the essentials and persist until they have achieved their objective. They are not reckless or inflexible, but they have a steely underlying will that endures through all changes in circumstance.

Most are also good at motivating their employees. They know how to articulate their vision and provide the right kind of leadership without stifling initiative. They hire able people, because they recognise that the quality of the team has a direct bearing on a company's success. Many have share-ownership schemes, because it pays to give employees an opportunity to benefit from future growth.

All ventures need a balance of talents. A small company must have a driving force, a manager, a sales director and a first-class accountant. Large corporations have departments, but there is always a danger that they will become too bureaucratic. Some entrepreneurs have tackled the problem by setting up units. Sir Richard Branson, for example, has a portfolio of companies. They all use the Virgin name but each operates in a different field. He maintains overall control, but gives them a lot of elbow room. Sir Martin Sorrell has built the largest advertising business in the world, mainly through acquisitions, but he also believes in allowing them to operate with the maximum possible freedom.

Thinking big

Visionary leaders 'think big'. They don't limit themselves to small dreams and ambitions. Their goal is to create an empire.

They don't expect to get there in a single leap, but they know what it takes to make a business grow.

People with lofty aims are experts at using OPM – Other People's Money. They often borrow staggering sums, but banks are not the only source of funds. Once a company has established an impressive track record, there are various other options. Venture capitalists and other financial institutions are always looking for entrepreneurs with big ideas and a plausible strategy. A common route is to float the business on the stock market, which not only raises capital but also makes it possible to use the shares for acquisitions.

Size isn't everything. Many companies have been brought low through careless expansion. In their headlong rush for growth they have assumed hair-raising risks, decimated their resources, and incurred vast debts. But there are many which have grown into large corporations because the leaders have stuck to what they know best.

In the 1970s and 80s, entrepreneurs like the late James Hanson created a new type of business – the conglomerate. This was a complex organisation with interests in many fields, from engineering to brick-making, textiles and tobacco. The people who ran them were in the business of 'industrial management' – of buying and developing companies to make them more successful. Hanson and other 'conglomateurs' became super-rich, but the concept fell out of favour because it lacked focus. The new emphasis was on 'unbundling' and 'demerging'. The founders were told that, if they wanted to get continued support, they had to return to 'core values'. In short, 'we like you to think big but we don't want you to ride madly off in all directions'.

Advice From the Rich

If you can dream it, you can do it.

Walt Disney

To improve a company fast, develop people fast.

Andrall Pearson, past president, Pepsico

Here lies a man who knew how to enlist the services of better men than himself.

tombstone of Andrew Carnegie

If you want to succeed, double your failure rate.

Thomas J. Watson, founder of IBM

No one can possibly achieve any real and lasting success by being a conformist.

J. Paul Getty

I have always believed businesses that concentrate on a very few core competencies will do the best. One of the lessons of the computer industry – as well as of life – is that it is almost impossible do everything well.

Bill Gates

There are many moments filled with despair and agony, when you have to fire people and cancel things and deal with very difficult situations. That's when you find out who you are and what your values are.

Steve Jobs on start-ups

It pays to be ignorant. If you're smart, you already know it can't be done.

Jeno Paulucci

It's better, I think, not to remember how much money you have, so you still have to work hard.

Y.K. Pao

How did I make my fortune? By always selling too soon. Sell, regret – and grow rich.

Nathan Rothschild

The first rule is not to lose money. The second rule is not to forget the first rule.

Warren Buffett

Never tell anyone what you are going to do until you have done it.

Cornelius Vanderbilt

If you see a bandwagon, it is too late.

Sir James Goldsmith

You can't build a reputation on what you are going to do.

Henry Ford

Work half days every day. It doesn't matter which half. The first twelve hours or the second twelve hours.

Kemmons Wilson, founder of Holiday Inns

You can have brilliant ideas, but if you can't get them across, your ideas won't get you anywhere.

Lee Iaccoca

Don't do anything someone else can do for you.

Bill Marriot, Sr.

The real secret of success is enthusiasm. Yes, more than enthusiasm I would say excitement. I like to see men get excited. When they get excited, they make a success of their lives.

An Wang

No matter how busy you are, you must take time to make the other person feel important.

Mary Kay Ash

The key to success is to get out into the store and listen to what the associates have to say. It's terribly important for everyone to get involved. Our best ideas come from clerks and stockboys.

Samuel Moore Walton, founder of Wal-Mart

Never acquire a business you don't know how to run.

Robert W. Johnson

Good fortune is what happens when opportunity meets with preparation.

Thomas Edison

Work only on problems that are manifestly important and seem to be nearly impossible to solve. That way you will have a natural market for your product and no competition.

Edwin Land, founder of Polaroid

I am grateful for all my problems. After each one was overcome, I became stronger and more able to meet those that were still to come. I grew in all my difficulties.

J.C. Penney

Only economically feasible products will become a reality. Where costs can be pushed down rapidly, great new vistas arise.

Robert Noyce, inventor of the silicon chip

Pessimism is a sickness you treat like any other sickness. The object is to get well as soon as possible, and get back to business.

Aristotle Onassis

Don't tell me how hard you work. Tell me how much you get done.

James Ling

The first five days of the week are when you work to keep up with the competition. It's on Saturdays and Sundays that you get ahead of them.

Curt Carlson

Never give up, and never under any circumstances deceive anybody. Have your word good.

Conrad Hilton

When you want something from a person, think first of what you can give him in return. Let him think that it's *he* who is coming off best. But at all times make sure that it's you in the end.

Harry Oppenheimer

If you want to succeed you should strike out on new paths rather than travel the worn paths of accepted status.

John D. Rockefeller

A leader has a vision and the conviction that a dream can be achieved. He inspires the power and energy to get it done.

Ralph Lauren

CHAPTER 19

MEGA TRENDS

How will the rich fare in coming decades? There have been so many dramatic upheavals in the past that it would plainly be unwise to take anything for granted. My grandfather was rich but lost everything in the Second World War.

I firmly believe that we Europeans will not fight each other again, but the same cannot be said for other parts of the world. The Middle East will remain turbulent, and many countries in Asia, Africa and what used to be the Soviet Union are also likely to be unstable. This, of course, is why so many of their rich have made substantial investments in Europe and the United States. They take the view that democratic societies like ours will always defend and protect individual rights. We do not confiscate assets unless it can be shown, in court, that they have been used to finance terrorism or other criminal activities.

When I wrote my first book on the rich, more than a quarter of a century ago, communism was still regarded as a major threat. We had already come close to war on several occasions. In America, many people were persecuted because they held left-wing views; they were said to be the 'enemy within'. The

US also got embroiled in a long and costly war in Vietnam, in an ultimately vain attempt to hold back the 'red tide'.

As we all know, the Soviet empire collapsed because a new generation of leaders, notably Mikhail Gorbachev, decided to change course. Today Russia and most of the other republics have embraced capitalism and have many millionaires of their own. The Berlin Wall has gone, Germany is again one country, and some of the former communist states have joined the European Union. It is a historic transformation, worth recalling because it showed that, given a choice, people would rather live in a free society than in one ruled by Marxists.

China still maintains a system that has been thoroughly discredited, but it may not do so for much longer. Recent years have seen growing pressure for radical change. Many Chinese are just as eager to get rich as people in Russia and the West. There are already ten known billionaires. The list is headed by Xu Rongmao, a former textile worker who controls more land than any private developer in America and Europe and builds luxury real estate projects that put even Donald Trump to shame for their sheer scale and flamboyance.

Another wealthy entrepreneur is Robin Li, the founder and chief executive of China's leading internet search engine. A native of Shanxi province to the west of Beijing, he went to the US for postgraduate study and worked for Dow in New Jersey and then Infoseek in Silicon Valley. When he returned home he started his own company, Baidu, in 2000. It now employs more than 700 people and is listed on Nasdaq; Li is reputedly worth $600 million. He says that for the time being he intends to concentrate on the domestic market but that he will eventually look outside.

He will not be the only one. Many Chinese already have substantial investments abroad, particularly in the United States and Canada. Hong Kong began the process when it was still a British colony, because it wasn't clear what would happen when it was handed over to Beijing. Many people acquired Canadian or British passports, as well as property and other assets, so they could leave if the communist regime made life difficult. Britain has a considerable number of rich Chinese – a fact not always recognised by the media because they like to keep a low profile. Their contacts with the nouveau riche in China give them a useful advantage.

The United States is a favourite target. Its insatiable appetite for cheap consumer goods has enabled China to accumulate a vast hoard of dollars, bonds and other paper which could be used to acquire control of US corporations.

India has also made rapid progress. There was a time when many Indians thought that communism was the answer to the country's daunting economic and social problems, but the revolution they so confidently predicted never happened – the government opted for socialism within a democratic framework. There were exchange controls and entrepreneurs had to cope with an abundance of red tape. This began to change in the early 1990s, and since then Indian governments have followed more liberal policies. The country now has a thriving middle class and many nouveau riche. A report published in 2005 by the National Council for Applied Economic Research, based in New Delhi, said that the number of *crorepatis* (India's rough equivalent of millionaires) has risen to an estimated 53,000 nationwide.

One of the best known is N.R. Narayana Murthy, sometimes referred to as the Indian Bill Gates. As a young man he was a firebrand socialist but later became a convert to private enterprise. He set up a software and information technology business with just $250 of capital, operating out of the bedroom of his modest house in Bombay. The company, Infosys, now employs 46,000 people and has an annual turnover of more than $2 billion. Murthy is a billionaire but says that he hates the ostentatious display of wealth – he and his wife still live in the three-bedroom house they moved into eighteen years ago. And Infosys pours millions into funds designed to help lepers, neglected children and burns victims. He told the *Guardian* in 2005: 'Capitalism can get India out of poverty, create more jobs, and furnish people with a level of disposable income they have never had before.' It is a view shared by many of the newly minted rich in Mumbai and the country's high-tech capital, Bangalore.

A CLASH OF CIVILISATIONS?

In America and other Western countries, fear of communism has been replaced by a new worry – the threat posed by Islamic fundamentalism. President Bush says that 9/11 changed the world and to some extent he is right. It certainly changed American attitudes. We all know what it led to: the invasion of Afghanistan and Iraq. I don't want to go over familiar ground, but there is one point that surely merits a place in a book on the rich – the claim that we are heading for a 'clash of civilisations'. This has been widely taken to mean that Muslims so strongly disapprove of our way of life, and every-thing we stand for, that a global conflict is inevitable. It is, of course, precisely what Osama Bin Laden and his cohorts have sought to bring about. It would be foolish to dismiss the argu-ment out of hand, but we need to keep a sense of perspective. Most Muslims in Europe (and, for that matter, America) are not religious fanatics who seek to impose their faith on us by force, and they are realistic enough to accept that attempts to create Islamic societies in the West are bound to fail. Tony Blair says that it would be more accurate to talk about a 'clash within a civilisation', which is what he believes will happen in the Middle East when the moderates decide to make a firm stand against the militant fundamentalists. We shall see.

George Bush maintains that the answer is 'regime change' – replacing dictatorships with democratically elected governments. A worthy aim, but it has so far proved harder than expected and it can't be taken for granted that new regimes will embrace Western values.

There is a widespread perception in the Muslim world that America's real motive is to control the oilfields and that it will resort to further military intervention to achieve its objectives. This is certainly the course advocated by the president's rich supporters and, if pursued, is bound to meet with a hostile response. (The next administration will, I hope, take a less aggressive view.)

Meanwhile, rich Westerners will find themselves increasingly targeted by terrorist groups as well as common criminals, especially if they go to Islamic countries, ignore their culture, and flaunt the trappings of their wealth.

THE 'TIME-BOMB'

There is another issue which troubles the rich in developed countries like ours – how, in the years ahead, governments are going to fund the welfare system they and their predecessors have created.

Much has been said and written about the 'demographic time-bomb', a fashionable term for what many economists predict will be a major cause of domestic strife in the 21st century. We have an ageing population, not only because of the remarkable increase in average life expectancy but also because of the decline in birth-rates. It isn't a 'blip' but a mega-trend. The elderly, it's said, will expect and demand the same benefits they have enjoyed since the end of the Second World War – and as their numbers rise, the cost of healthcare and pensions will explode. A shrinking number of young people will have to shoulder a growing burden and at some stage there will be an 'age war' or, if you prefer the phrase used by Tony Blair in a different context, a 'clash within a civilisation'.

There are several things wrong with this alarming thesis, quite apart from the possibility that a nuclear war could make it irrelevant. Firstly, it assumes that we are all dependent on state support. Many of us can afford to make our own arrangements and are already doing so – recent years have seen significant growth in private healthcare. Secondly, it ignores the fact that many older people are prepared to continue working, and pay taxes, providing they are given the opportunity. It is perverse to whinge about the 'burden' and, at the same time, seek to shove them out of the workforce as soon as possible. The young can't have it both ways. Thirdly, we could have many more taxpayers if we welcomed skilled immigrants instead of complaining that there is 'no more room'.

If there is to be an age war, you and I would naturally want to be on the winning side. But what form is this conflict supposed to take? Rebellions tend to be led by students and trade unions, but a fight with the elderly is unlikely to command much public sympathy and politicians will be reluctant to offend the fastest-growing sector of the electorate.

Ministers say that they are concerned about future generations, but this is a dubious claim. Governments seldom look beyond the next general election, so they usually come up with quick fixes. There is an endless stream of pledges and eye-catching gimmicks which never add up to anything with shape or vision. This particular time-bomb is a long-term problem, so why alienate voters by dealing with it *now*? Economists say that it will *have* to be addressed in the near future and, not surprisingly, one of their proposals is that the government should 'soak the rich'. It appeals to politicians because, according to polls, most people still believe that they can pay for everything. Labour MPs prefer to talk about the 'redistribution of wealth', but no one is fooled by the euphemism. What needs to be more clearly understood is that a vast chunk of the 'redistributed' money is squandered on maintaining a bloated bureaucracy.

In France, a socialist government introduced a wealth tax some years ago. Many left-wing politicians in Britain would like to see a similar tax here, but the French experience has shown that it doesn't solve the problem. This is also the conclusion reached by various British committees who have investigated the issue. They decided that administrative cost would be so high that the net gain to the Exchequer would be very modest.

Governments on both sides of the Atlantic are taking a hard line on tax evasion, and rightly so, but any attempt to revive the confiscatory taxes we had in the 1960s and 70s would be as counter-productive as they were then. If Gordon Brown is serious about creating an 'enterprise culture' he will have to keep that in mind.

Winston Churchill once said that 'for a nation to try to tax itself into prosperity is like a man standing in a bucket and trying to lift himself up by the handle'. Margaret Thatcher shared his view, though she did not express it so wittily. She firmly rejected the notion that the answer to everything is for the state to spend and intervene more. She was a pragmatist who didn't mind being reviled if that was the price for rescuing the country from the dread grip of the trade unions and the incompetent civil servants who were running so much of British industry. Her tax cuts and programme of privatisation (since widely copied around the world) invigorated the economy.

There was a storm of abuse when she was quoted as telling a woman's magazine that 'there is no such thing as society'. The remark still turns up in newspaper columns, and even in

247

speeches made by some Tory politicians, so let me remind the critics of what she went on to say: 'There are individual men and women, and there are families. And no government can do anything except through people, and people must look after themselves first. It's our duty to look after ourselves and then to look after our neighbour.'

In her subsequent autobiography, *The Downing Street Years*, she explained that the error she was objecting to was the confusion of society with the state as the helper of first resort. The poor had to be helped but it had to be help of very different kinds if public spending was not just going to reinforce a dependency culture. She added: 'I was an individualist in the sense that I believed that individuals are ultimately accountable for their actions and must behave like it.' You may disagree with her stance, but remember that she won three general elections, which would not have happened if a majority of voters had found it unacceptable. I certainly felt that she was on the right track and contributed to some of her speeches. I expect that we shall hear more about the need to 'look after ourselves' in the years ahead.

A major question for all of us is what our savings will buy in the future. We have seen what inflation can do. It creates an *illusion* of wealth, which is why so many people underrate its damaging effects. They think they are better off than they really are.

In Germany, during the 1920s, money lost so much value that people had to pay billions of marks for bread. More recently, countries in Latin America have struggled with inflation of more than 100 per cent. Britain has never had to go through anything like that, but the 1970s were bad enough. At one time it hit 27 per cent, which was particularly hard on pensioners. They thought they had made reasonable provision for what they hoped would be a comfortable old age, and were cruelly disappointed.

Western governments have become better at curbing inflation, so it may seem that there is no need to worry. But Britain cannot expect to be isolated from global trends, such as rising prices for oil and raw materials. And it remains to be seen what our government's massive public spending commitments will lead to.

As the private bank Coutts has pointed out, a million pounds buys five times less than it did 25 years ago. No one really knows what it will buy 25 years from now, but it seems prudent to assume that it will continue to lose value.

The 'wealth management industry' offers a wide choice of protection – gold, silver, shares, land, paintings, antique furniture and even stamps. There are dealers who tell people that, if they want a hedge against inflation, they should go for pop memorabilia, classic cars, and teddy bears. The *very* rich can easily afford to do all of those things, and are seldom concerned about the risks. Auction houses like Sotheby's frequently sell works of art for staggering sums. Paintings by Picasso and Van Gogh have gone for £50 million or more, and I doubt if the buyers were interested only in acquiring a hedge.

I have always believed that the best investment most of us can make is our own home. I still do, but there is no automatic correlation between inflation rates and property values. The idea that you can't lose money if you buy property is as much of a myth as the notion that you can't lose money buying art. Ask all the people who bought homes in the 1980s and then saw an alarming drop in prices. As with all investments, it's very much a matter of making the right choices at the right time.

CAPITAL GAINS

One of the great strengths of liberal capitalism is its ability to change and adapt without destroying the freedoms which most people regard as so vitally important in terms of personal happiness. Western societies have been transformed to an extent that seemed utopian 100 or even 50 years ago.

For centuries the rich saw no need to concern themselves with the by-products of their business ventures. The Industrial Revolution brought Britain great wealth and power, but it also brought smokestack industries which polluted the air and rivers. The landscape was disfigured by numerous factories and mills, and cities were blanketed in fog. Waste was dumped without any thought of the consequences.

Capitalism no longer functions that way. We now have an unprecedented range of laws designed to protect the environment, and business leaders accept that they have new and wider responsibilities. The air and rivers are cleaner and urban renewal projects have transformed derelict areas in many parts of the country. There are more green spaces, more business parks, more recreational facilities. Waterfront warehouses have been turned into smart apartment blocks, museums, offices or shopping areas. Service industries have become more important than manufacturing, and there is more respect for the rights and welfare of employees.

All this has made fortunes for a new generation of entrepreneurs and in the years ahead there will be many more opportunities to get rich through innovative ventures. A big idea often has any number of small ideas within it, waiting to be discovered. Computers are an obvious example.

I have no doubt that we shall see further significant advances in technology and services. Many will come from large corporations but there will also be ample scope for independent small firms. Promising fields include waste management, home insulation, air conditioning, fish farming, desalination, genetic engineering and renewable sources of energy, such as solar power. Improved battery technology will create a genuine public demand for electric cars. (If you think this is fanciful, remember that not so long ago personal computers and mobile phones were also dismissed as gadgets with very limited appeal.)

It is private enterprise that will be mainly responsible for creating the wealth that politicians are so eager to distribute. This also goes for many other parts of the world. There are several types of capitalism: the American version is different from that of Europe and of countries like India. But all have this in common: they involve a substantial and growing degree of private ownership.

Another welcome development is the willingness of corporations and wealthy individuals to help the poor in less fortunate countries. A prominent example is the decision by Bill Gates and Warren Buffett, the two richest men on the planet, to join forces in a campaign to tackle global poverty and disease. The sums of money involved are huge – they have committed themselves to spending $60 billion. Sir Tom Hunter, the Scottish retail entrepreneur and richest man in Scotland, has put £55 million of his own money into an initiative with former US president Clinton: they aim to improve water and sanitation, health, agriculture and education in Africa. Carlos Slim Helu, the third richest man in the world, is ploughing some of his wealth into a campaign to alleviate poverty in Latin America. There are many other examples.

I have tried to show, in this book, how much depends on one's attitude. I admire people with a spirit of adventure, and I strongly defend the right of individuals to do their own thing within the framework of the law. I accept that capitalism still has many flaws, but in its present form it is vastly superior to communism and other authoritarian systems of government. I do not envy the rich, because envy is deeply unattractive and often self-destructive. I know that success should not be measured solely in terms of money, but I believe that people should be allowed to enjoy the financial rewards that come with talent, determination, willingness to take risks, and achievement.

ACKNOWLEDGEMENTS

I have interviewed many people for this book. Some have talked to me in the full knowledge that they would be quoted: others have wanted to remain anonymous and I have respected their wishes.

I have also used many other sources, including newspapers, magazines, websites, autobiographies and biographies, radio and TV interviews, and speeches made by super-rich entrepreneurs at seminars and conferences. There are no footnotes, because I did not set out to produce an academic study, but I have mentioned the source when I felt it would be churlish not to do so.

Much of journalism is here today and gone tomorrow; some of us write books because we believe that the best merits a longer shelf-life.

A great deal of effort has gone into checking and cross-checking all the facts. It wasn't easy, because so many of the rich prefer to keep their affairs secret and because some, especially the nouveau riche, tend to exaggerate their achievements and wealth. The statements they make, or are made on their behalf, often turn out to be self-serving and unreliable.

253

As with all non-fiction books that deal with the present as well as the past, there is also a risk that events will change what one has written in good faith.

I am grateful to my publisher, Peter Pugh, and his excellent team at Icon (notably Oliver Pugh and Duncan Heath) for the help they have given me with the research, and to my wife, Sylvette, for putting up with the strain I have imposed on her and for the valuable contribution she has made. Any mistakes you may have identified are my own.

INDEX

Beckham, David 93–4, 165, 222
Beckham, Victoria 94, 222
Beetles, Chris 145
Belgravia 19
Benedict XVI, Pope 171
Berezovsky, Boris 66, 67
Berkshire Hathaway 111
Bezos, Jeff 53–5
Bhs 56, 57, 58
Bill & Melinda Gates Foundation
    45, 113–14, 221
billionaires, dollar 11
Bin Laden, Osama 33, 244
Bipartisan Campaign Reform Act 185
Black, Conrad 189
Blair, Tony 4, 79, 171, 186, 244
Blake, Quentin 145
Blenheim Palace 136
Bloomberg, Michael (Mike)
    108–9, 185
Body Shop 18, 38, 234
Boesky, Ivan 129–30, 132
books, self-help 226, 227
botox injections 195–6
bounty hunters 218
boxing 94–5
Branson, Richard 60–3
  hot air balloons 158
  island retreat 140
  portfolio of companies 235
  space tour venture 155
  TV series 120
bribery 170, 186
Brin, Sergey 52–3
British Airways 62
British style 17
Broackes, Nigel 116–17, 153
Brown, Gordon 4, 247
Brunei, Sultan of 33, 151
Bruno, Frank 95
Bucellati, Antonio 124
Buckingham Palace 146, 148
Buffett, Howard 109–10
Buffett, Warren 109–14, 238, 251
burglary 198
Burton, Richard 163

Bush, Barbara 134
Bush, George H. 134
Bush, George W. 32, 170, 185, 245
Busson, Arki 222–3

Cadabra 54
Caine, Michael 83–4
Camilla, Duchess of Cornwall 29,
    146, 149
Caparo Group 76
capitalism 3, 249–52
Capone, Al 124, 200
Caring, Richard 57, 77, 147
Carl Gustav, King of Sweden 26
Carlson, Curt 239–40
Carnegie, Andrew 221, 237
Carphone Warehouse 230–2
carriages 150
cars 150–1
  electric 251
Carter, Jimmy 168, 201
Carter, Rosalynn 168
casinos 148, 160–2
Cats 87–8, 89
Cattelan, Maurizio 145
Cayman Islands 126, 128
change 41–2
charity, bequests to 220–1
charity auctions 222–3
Charles, Prince of Wales 28–9,
    146, 149
Chatwal, Vikram 148
Chelsea FC 67–8
Chicago Bulls 102
China 35, 242
Chukotka 67
Church Commissioners 172–3
Church of England 172–3
Churchill, Winston 152, 187, 247
Citizen Kane 137
City, the 103–4
City Centre Properties 115–16
civilisations, clash of 244–5
Clapton, Eric 222
class roles 17
Cleopatra 194

INDEX